Start Your Own

CLEANING SERVICE

WITHDRAWN

Additional titles in *Entrepreneur's* Startup Series

Start Your Own

Arts and Crafts Business
Automobile Detailing Business
Bar and Club
Bed and Breakfast
Blogging Business
Business on eBay
Car Wash
Child-Care Service
Cleaning Service
Clothing Store and More
Coaching Business
Coin-Operated Laundry
Construction and Contracting Business
Consulting Business
Day Spa and More
e-Business
Event Planning Business
Executive Recruiting Business
Fashion Accessories Business
Florist Shop and Other Floral Businesses
Food Truck Business
Freelance Writing Business and More
Freight Brokerage Business
Gift Basket Service
Grant-Writing Business
Graphic Design Business
Green Business

Hair Salon and Day Spa
Home Inspection Service
Import/Export Business
Information Marketing Business
Kid-Focused Business
Lawn Care or Landscaping Business
Mail Order Business
Medical Claims Billing Service
Net Services Business
Online Coupon or Daily Deal Business
Online Education Business
Personal Concierge Service
Personal Training Business
Pet Business and More
Pet-Sitting Business and More
Photography Business
Public Relations Business
Restaurant and More
Retail Business and More
Self-Publishing Business
Seminar Production Business
Senior Services Business
Travel Business and More
Tutoring and Test Prep Business
Vending Business
Wedding Consultant Business
Wholesale Distribution Business

Entrepreneur
MAGAZINE'S

startup

4TH EDITION

Start Your Own

CLEANING SERVICE

Maid Service • Janitorial Service
Carpet and Upholstery Service
and More

Entrepreneur Press and Jacquelyn Lynn

EP
Entrepreneur
PRESS®

Entrepreneur Press, Publisher
Cover Design: Beth Hansen-Winter
Production and Composition: Eliot House Productions

This publication is designed to provide accurate and authoritative information in regard to the subject matter covered. It is sold with the understanding that the publisher is not engaged in rendering legal, accounting or other professional services. If legal advice or other expert assistance is required, the services of a competent professional person should be sought.

Library of Congress Cataloging-in-Publication Data
Lynn, Jacquelyn.
    Start your own cleaning business/by Entrepreneur Press and Jacquelyn Lynn.—4e [ed.].
      pages cm.—(Startup)
    Includes index.
    ISBN-13: 978-1-59918-528-6 (alk. paper)
    ISBN-10: 1-59918-528-8 (alk. paper)
    1. Building cleaning industry—Management. 2. House cleaning—Management.
3. New business enterprises—Management. I. Entrepreneur Press. II. Title.
HD9999.B882L96 2014
648'.50681—dc23   2013047271

Contents

Preface xi

Chapter 1
An Introduction to Cleaning Services 1
    The Driving Forces 2

Chapter 2
Startup and Operations 7
    What Are the Qualifications? 9
    Predictable? Yes and No 10
    Franchise or Independent Operation? 12
    Buying an Existing Business 12

Chapter 3
Residential Cleaning Service 15
    Who Are Your Customers? 16
        Beyond Individual Homes 18
    Who Are Your Competitors? 19
    Equipment 19
    Supplies 21
    Standard Operations 22

What Will You Clean? 22
How Will You Clean? 23
Scheduling 25
What Does a Typical Day Include? 25
From That First Phone Call 26
Maintaining Customer Records 28
Pitfalls.. 30
Oops! 32

Chapter 4
Janitorial Service **39**
Who Are Your Customers? 40
Who Are Your Competitors? 41
Equipment 42
Floor Cleaning Equipment 43
Chemicals.. 44
Standard Operations 44
Laundry 48
Maintaining Customer Records 48
Bidding.. 48
Estimating a Job.................................... 50
Be Prepared to Answer Questions 53
Cash Flow Issue 54
Security... 55

Chapter 5
Carpet and Upholstery Cleaning Services **59**
Who Are Your Customers? 60
Who Are Your Competitors? 60
Equipment 61
Cleaning Methods 62
Chemicals... 64
Carpet Cleaning Basics 65
Carpet Cleaning Specifics 68
Handling the Initial Service Request 68
Visiting the Customer's Home 68
Writing the Invoice 69
Performing the Service 70
Furniture Cleaning Specifics 70

Inspecting Furniture Before Giving an Estimate 70
Writing Your Estimate 72
Cleaning Furniture 72
Cleaning Drapes 73

Chapter 6
Other Cleaning Businesses 75
Window Cleaning 76
Disaster Cleaning and Restoration 77
Blind Cleaning 77
Pressure Washing. 78
Restroom Cleaning 78
Chimney Sweeping 79
Ceiling and Wall Cleaning 79
Post Death and Trauma Cleaning. 81

Chapter 7
Developing Your Plan. 83
Business Plan Elements 84
To Market, To Market. 85
Are You on a Mission? 87

Chapter 8
Structuring Your Business 91
Naming Your Company. 92
Trademarks. 93
Protect Your Mark. 94
Legal Structure 94
Licenses and Permits 95
Professional Services 97
Create Your Own Advisory Board 99
Insurance Issues 101
Deliveries and Storage. 101

Chapter 9
Money Matters. 103
Sources of Startup Funds. 104
Setting Prices 105
Labor and Materials 106

▲

Overhead 106
Profit 107
Setting Residential Cleaning Service Prices. 107
Setting Janitorial Service Prices 108
Setting Carpet Cleaning Prices. 109
Keeping Records 110
Billing 111
Establishing Credit Policies 113
Red Flags 113
Accepting Credit and Debit Cards 114

Chapter 10
Setting Up Your Business **117**
The Homebased Tax Advantage 118
The Commercial Option. 119
Vehicles. 119
Build a Fleet. 121
Check Out the Drivers 121

Chapter 11
Human Resources **123**
What Makes a Good Cleaning Service Employee? 124
Look In the Right Places. 125
Evaluating Applicants 127
Take Care of Your Employees. 128
Now That They're Hired 129
Training Techniques 130
Uniforms 132
Employee Benefits 132
Child Labor Laws 133
What Should You Pay? 135
Employee Theft. 135
When You Suspect a Problem. 136

Chapter 12
Purchasing **139**
Choosing Suppliers 140
Buying Supplies 141
Dealing with Suppliers. 143

Suppliers Are Also Creditors 143
Negotiating a Deal 143

Chapter 13

Equipment **145**
Basic Office Equipment 146
Telecommunications 148
Telephone 149
Answering Machine/Voice Mail 150
Cell Phone 150
Toll-Free Number 151
Email 151
The Best Equipment Is Information 151

Chapter 14

Marketing **153**
Researching and Defining Your Market 154
Communicating with Your Market 155
What About Your Website? 158
The Elements of Image 159
Trade Shows 160
Trade Show Tips 162

Chapter 15

Tales from the Trenches **163**
Never Stop Learning 164
Tap All Your Resources 164
Clean It Like It's Your Own 164
Develop Systems 164
Be Careful! 164
Don't Undersell Yourself 165
Take Care of Your Employees 165
Prepare for the Worst 165
Watch Your Chemical Combos 165
Find a Niche 165
Develop Your Computer Skills 166
Track Labor Costs 166
Invest in Customer Service 166
Keep Your Eye on the Economy 167

Don't Take Every Job 167

Appendix
Cleaning Services Resources **169**
    Associations 169
    Consultants and Other Experts. 171
    Credit Card Services 172
    Equipment and Supply Sources. 172
    Franchise and Business Opportunities 173
    Internet and Government Resources 175
    Magazines and Publications. 175
    Successful Cleaning Services. 176

Glossary **179**

Index **181**

Preface

Have you ever stopped to think about how much time you spend cleaning things? Your house, your car, your clothes—the list goes on and on. And how often have you wished there were some magic way to get your cleaning chores done so you could move on to the activities you really enjoy?

That mind-set is behind one of the most lucrative and recession-resistant industries in America: cleaning. Certainly you look at cleaning in a less-than-enchanted light as you're toiling through your own kitchen and bathrooms on a Saturday when you'd rather be going to the movies. But mopping, vacuuming, and polishing all take on quite a different connotation when they're the foundation for a business that can provide you with a secure financial future. That business is a cleaning service, and the industry is rich with a variety of markets ranging from residential to industrial, from basic to high-tech.

Regardless of the industry niche you choose, one of the appealing aspects of a cleaning service is the opportunity for repeat business—when things get cleaned, they usually get dirty and have to be re-cleaned. It's a wonderful, inevitable cycle that means regular revenue for a cleaning business.

You may already know what type of cleaning business you want to start, or you may still be exploring your options. This book will give you the information and tools you need to start a residential cleaning service, a commercial janitorial service, and a carpet cleaning business. It will also introduce you to a variety of specialty cleaning services that will work as independent operations or adjuncts to another cleaning business.

This guide is structured to take you step-by-step, starting with your decision to start a cleaning service through running a successful, profitable operation. It begins with an introduction to the industry, a look at how successful operators got their starts, and some basic business planning elements. Next, it looks at specific types of cleaning services, including a residential cleaning service, janitorial service, carpet and upholstery cleaning service, and other specialty cleaning businesses. Then it discusses various startup and operational issues, such as your legal structure, insurance, location, vehicles, personnel, purchasing, equipment, and financial management.

It's a good idea to read every chapter in this book, whether you think it applies to the particular business you want to start or not. For example, even if you're planning to start a residential cleaning service, you may pick up some good ideas from the chapters on janitorial and carpet cleaning services. And when you read about other cleaning businesses, you may decide to offer similar services.

Because the best information about business comes from people who are already in the trenches, we interviewed successful cleaning service business owners who were happy to share their stories. Their experience spans all types of cleaning service operations, and several of them are examples themselves of how to blend more than one type of operation into a successful business. Throughout the book, you'll read about what works—and doesn't—for these folks, and how you can use their techniques in your own business.

You'll also learn what the cleaning service business is really like. The hours can be flexible, but they're usually long. The profit margins are good, but only if you're paying attention to detail. The market is tremendous, but you'll have a substantial amount of competition, which means you need a plan to set yourself apart.

Like anything else, there's no quick path to success. The cleaning service business takes hard work, dedication, and commitment. It's not glamorous; in fact, one of the biggest challenges you'll face is the industry's menial image. But by investing your time, energy, and resources, you can be the one who is truly cleaning up, both literally and figuratively.

An Introduction to Cleaning Services

No matter what it is, if it can get dirty, chances are someone will be willing to pay you to clean it. And that's why few industries can claim the variety and depth of opportunities that professional cleaning can.

The cleaning industry has two primary market groups: consumer and commercial. The consumer arena consists primarily of residential cleaning services (traditionally known as maid services), along with carpet cleaners, window cleaners, and a variety of other cleaning services required on a less frequent basis. The commercial arena is dominated by janitorial services, which typically provide a wider range of services than residential services, along with other cleaning companies, such as carpet and window cleaners, that target businesses rather than individual consumers. While it's recommended that you decide on a niche and concentrate on building a business that will serve your chosen market, it's entirely realistic to expect to be able to serve multiple markets successfully.

With all this opportunity, what does the competition look like? Glance through your telephone directory or do a local internet search—the number of cleaning services may make you think the market is already flooded and there's no room for you. That's not true.

First, anyone can list in the Yellow Pages just by having a business telephone line. A mere listing doesn't mean the company is offering quality service to the market you're targeting. Anyone can get on the internet by setting up a website. And while a website is an important part of being in business today, simply having a website doesn't mean you have a competitive business.

Second, the demand for cleaning services is tremendous. Plenty of residential cleaning companies have waiting lists for clients because they simply can't serve the entire market. Many carpet cleaners and other types of specialized cleaning services aren't full-time operations and therefore don't offer serious competition. And a significant number of janitorial services are mom-and-pop operations run by people who want just enough work to earn a living.

Third, cleaning service customers want quality, and many operators are unable to deliver that. Ask anyone who has ever hired a company to clean something in their home or office if they've had any bad experiences, and chances are you'll hear some nightmarish stories of poor-quality work, damage to property, and even theft.

If you offer quality service, operate with integrity, and charge reasonable prices, you'll be a success in a cleaning service business.

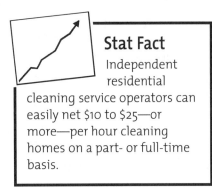

Stat Fact

Independent residential cleaning service operators can easily net $10 to $25—or more—per hour cleaning homes on a part- or full-time basis.

The Driving Forces

Shifting demographics and changing lifestyles are driving the surge in residential cleaning businesses. Busy consumers don't have the time or inclination to clean for themselves; they want to spend their limited leisure hours doing things they enjoy, so they're looking for personal support in the form of housecleaning services, lawn maintenance, errand-running services, and more. They want someone else to handle these tasks, and they want them done well.

The service providers in these areas that will thrive will be the ones with an emphasis on quality and personal service. "Every one of my customers is different and special, and I treat them that way," says Wanda Guzman, owner of Guzman Commercial Cleaning in Orlando. Guzman began her business as a residential cleaning service and expanded to commercial accounts. "It's a relationship—I take care of them, and they are loyal to me."

On the commercial side, the dual trends of outsourcing and niche businesses are behind the growing number of janitorial and specialty cleaning services. Businesses need to have their offices and plants cleaned, but it doesn't always make sense for

> **Stat Fact**
>
> There are an estimated 1.4 million maids and housekeeping cleaners in the United States, according to the Bureau of Labor Statistics, and about 12 percent of them are self-employed.

Polishing the Industry's Image

The cleaning services industry provides a critical service to both individuals and commercial enterprises. It requires hard work, professionalism, and an awareness of evolving technologies and information. Yet it suffers from an image problem. What's the solution?

The first step to improving the industry's image is developing a higher level of self-esteem in the participants. The positive results of properly done commercial cleaning include providing a safe, healthy indoor environment for workers and helping people avoid symptoms and illnesses caused by unhealthy environments. Every person on your staff needs to understand the value of the work they do.

Another critical element in industry image is appearance. Cleaners who are well-groomed and wear neat, professional-looking uniforms elevate not only their own personal self-esteem but the image of their company and the entire industry.

Finally, it's important that everyone in the organization, from the front-line cleaning staff to senior management, work to continuously increase their knowledge and enhance their skills. This means comprehensive training at both basic and advanced levels, using a variety of learning techniques.

Bright Idea

Restaurants are a strong market for contract cleaners. By the time cooks and servers have worked their shifts, they're tired and not inclined to do a good job cleaning. Of course, your performance must meet applicable health codes, and the work is often done either very late at night or early in the morning, but the opportunity is substantial.

them to employ their own cleaning staffs. Nor does it make sense for them to own the equipment and expertise necessary for jobs such as carpet shampooing, which are done infrequently.

"We're not just a cleaning company," says Mike Blair, owner of AAA Prestige Carpet Care in St. George, Utah. "It's not just about pushing a wand or running a machine. It's not just kicking the dirt out. It's a matter of taking good care of people."

This is good news for an entrepreneur who is more interested in building a solid, profitable business than in conquering new horizons.

Before you leap into the cleaning business, it's important to look at it with 20/20 vision. Though technology certainly impacts cleaning services, this isn't a high-tech business. Nor is there any glitz to it. And there will be times when you'll have as much trouble as comedian Rodney Dangerfield had getting respect.

The upside is that you can build a profitable business that will generate revenue quickly. Most cleaning service businesses can be operated on either a part- or full-time basis, either from home or from a commercial location. That flexibility gives this industry a strong appeal to a wide range of people with a variety of goals.

Another positive aspect of the industry is that within each category of cleaning businesses are market niches and operating styles that vary tremendously. Michael W. Ray, owner of Pro Building Services Inc. in Salt Lake City, says, "We offer a wide range of services to a very limited clientele. We have refined our customer base to a group that we feel we can best serve in a way that will allow us to maintain those customers permanently."

This means you can build a company that suits your individual style and talents. If you like doing the work yourself, you can stay small and do so. If your skills are more administrative and supervisory in nature, you can build and manage teams to do the work. For people who like working outside, the opportunities in service areas such as window cleaning and pressure washing are abundant. Residential cleaning services offer fairly predictable hours; disaster restoration and cleanup can mean calls at all hours of the day or night.

Smart Tip

Start small; test your market and operation slowly before expanding. Small mistakes are easier to correct than large ones.

Stat Fact
The number of building clean-ing workers is expected to grow 11 percent between 2010 and 2020, which is the average for all occupations, according to the Bureau of Labor Statistics. Many of the new jobs will be in facilities related to health care.

Few industries offer this tremendous range of choices and opportunities, and the need for general and niche cleaning is expected to increase in the future. To help you find your place in this thriving field, let's take a look at the day-to-day operations of some typical cleaning businesses.

Startup
and Operations

Ask school-age youngsters what they want to do when they grow up and chances are slim they'll say they want to be in the cleaning business. But when you talk to the owners of successful cleaning businesses, they're full of enthusiasm about their chosen profession.

Most took a roundabout path to owning and running their businesses. For example, prior to starting her residential cleaning service in Orlando, Fenna Owens worked in the service department of a transportation company, and before that, she owned an automotive business that specialized in replacing brakes. In her personal life, she had used the same cleaning person for eight years and was pleased with her work. But when her cleaning person relocated and Owens had to hire someone else to do the job, she realized how challenging it was to find a quality service.

"I was paying somebody every week to clean my house, and if I put my finger on the mantel, I found dust," she recalls. "I was also not really happy with my job. I had enjoyed working for myself [with the brake business]. So I started telling my friends that I was going to start a cleaning business, and some of them said to come to their house."

Another residential cleaning service operator we talked to had been a preschool teacher and gymnastics instructor. She started her cleaning business when her marriage ended and she needed more money than she was making. Still another admits she had no job skills, and cleaning was all she knew how to do—so after working for an established company for a while, she left and started her own business.

Michael Ray started his janitorial service, Pro Building Services Inc. in Salt Lake City, to support himself and his family while he was working on a college degree in public relations. He had been a custodian for another company, where he was encouraged to start his own business by one of the vendor's sales representatives. So, with an investment of less than $400, he took the seats out of his Volkswagen Beetle, loaded it up with equipment and supplies (including an old buffer his father-in-law gave him), and went looking for clients. His first customer was a small independent grocery store, and he did all the work himself. After he graduated from college, he decided he didn't want to work in the public relations field; he wanted to continue operating the company he already owned. Today, his janitorial service employs more than 100 people.

Mike Blair was teaching at a college and doing some consulting work when he met someone with a carpet cleaning business for sale. He bought the business and realized he enjoyed being an entrepreneur. When he decided to move his family to St. George, Utah, there was no question that he would start another carpet cleaning company. He decided to buy new equipment for the new operation, and his startup capital consisted of $25,000, which he borrowed using the equity in his home.

Today's cleaning industry attracts people from all walks of life with a wide range of skills and experience and an even wider range of available capital. It's truly a something-for-everyone business.

What Are the Qualifications?

The necessary qualifications depend, of course, on the type of cleaning service you decide to start. But for any type of service business, you need the determination to make the business work, a willingness to please the customer, and the dedication to provide a thorough cleaning job.

Many residential cleaning business operators are perfectionists. A significant number of them were prompted to start their own companies after unpleasant and unfortunate experiences with other services, taking an "I-can-do-it-better,-so-I-may-as-well-make-money-at-it" attitude.

Another critical requirement for the owner and the employees of any type of cleaning service is honesty. "Clients must have total trust in the people who come to clean their homes," says Owens. This is important, whether they're cleaning bathrooms every week, carpets twice a year, or dusting and vacuuming an office at night.

A residential cleaning service is probably the simplest business in terms of necessary cleaning skills. Janitorial services, carpet cleaning businesses, and other niche

Privacy Act

Regardless of the type of cleaning business you start, chances are you'll have the opportunity to learn very personal things about your customers.

"I am not there to read anything; I am there to clean the house," says Orlando residential cleaning service owner Fenna Owens. "If anyone leaves delicate papers out, or anything else laying around, they don't have to worry about it, because I'm not going to stand still and read it. It's not mine, and it's none of my business."

If you accidentally find out sensitive information, never repeat it. "Don't ever talk about your customers to other customers, especially if they know each other," says Owens. "It's nobody's business what they have in their house."

Wanda Guzman, who operates a combined residential and commercial cleaning service also in Orlando, agrees. "When you're cleaning, you're in the most private part of someone's home. People have to feel safe that you're going to keep their confidence," she says. "Sometimes in offices people will leave important papers and files out. When that happens, my policy is don't look, don't touch."

cleaning operations often require the use of special equipment and/or cleaning solutions for which you must be trained.

Beyond actually being able to do the work, a cleaning service operator needs some basic business skills. You need to understand the administrative requirements of running a company, you should be able to manage your time efficiently, and you must be able to build relationships with your employees and your customers.

None of the requirements of being a cleaning business owner are highly complex, nor do they require anything more than average intelligence. Many successful cleaning businesses were started on a shoestring, with just a few dollars' worth of supplies and plenty of energy and enthusiasm. Of course, if you have capital available, your options are greater.

Predictable? Yes and No

The level of predictability in the cleaning business depends on your particular operation and clientele. With a residential or janitorial service, most of your business will be long-term contracts, where you're cleaning the same home or business on a regular basis. You'll likely do some one-time jobs, or occasionally do extra things for existing customers, but the bulk of your business will be on a routine schedule.

Carpet cleaners have plenty of repeat customers, but not at the same level of predictability as residential and janitorial services. The frequency of service is significantly less, since most consumers have their carpets cleaned one to three times a year, and businesses typically only slightly more often. Also, when the economy contracts, many customers will opt to extend the time between carpet cleanings.

For most types of cleaning service businesses, the best business is repeat business—in fact, for many, it's the only business. Repeat customers will make up 75 to 90 percent of your accounts. This is the bread-and-butter of the industry, since one-time-only cleanings bring you one-time-only income. It's up to you to turn these one-time jobs into repeat customers.

If you do a one-time cleaning as a residential or janitorial service, follow up with a telephone call one or two days after your visit to find out how the customer liked your service. Then tell the customer about your regular

> **Tip...**
>
> **Smart Tip**
> Let your employees know you expect them to be polite and friendly, but they should avoid getting into long conversations with customers. They're there to work, not to talk—and if they're going to stay on schedule, they don't have time for a lot of chitchat.

On With the Show

Regardless of what part of the cleaning industry you're in, trade shows and conventions are an excellent source of information. Exhibitors are eager to show off their latest products and show you how these items can enhance your business. For many homebased business owners, these shows may be your only opportunity to meet face-to-face with a sizable number of prospective suppliers and customers in a short time.

Check with industry trade and professional associations, as well as your suppliers, for information about upcoming shows. Ask for a list of exhibitors in advance so you can decide ahead of time which companies you want to contact. Keep an open mind while at the show, because you may find an unexpected sales or productivity tool. And if necessary, be willing to travel to attend the right show; it could be one of the best investments of time and money you make for your business.

You can choose from large, national shows sponsored by associations (for a list of associations, see this book's Appendix) to smaller, regional shows that are often sponsored by manufacturers. Mike Blair, owner of AAA Prestige Carpet Care in St. George, Utah, recommends both types of trade shows to get a true picture of what's going on in the industry and what all your resources are.

---

cleaning programs. Be friendly and gracious even if the customer says no. They may call you when they need a one-time job again, or they may change their minds about regular service at some future point.

If you do carpet cleaning or another type of cleaning that typically isn't done frequently, set up a system to remind customers when their next service should be performed, whether it's annually, semiannually, or quarterly. They may not think to call you, but if you call them, they'll most likely schedule a cleaning.

Some cleaning service businesses are strongly seasonal; others are not. Janitorial services are probably the most stable in terms of volume, unless they have customers in seasonal businesses. Residential services tend to enjoy a fairly consistent volume year-round, with perhaps some extra one-time-only cleanings around the winter holidays and some additional spring cleaning requests when the weather begins to warm up. Carpet cleaning services are typically busier in the spring and summer, with volume dropping in the fall and becoming very light in the winter. The seasonality of other types of cleaning services depends on what's being cleaned and the climate of the region in which clients are located.

Franchise or Independent Operation?

It's an advantage that franchises will work closely with you as you start your business and take it to the point where it's running smoothly and profitably, especially in the beginning. But you may find that once you become established and are financially secure, a franchise agreement is a decided disadvantage.

A franchise is the way to go for people who want to own their own business but would rather choose an opportunity that has proved successful for many others rather than gamble on developing their own system. Also, most franchises provide a degree of marketing support—particularly in the area of national advertising and name recognition—that's difficult for individuals to match.

In the long run, you'll likely invest far less money operating as an independent service than as part of a franchise. Also, as an independent, you're not tied to any pre-established

> **Tip...**
>
> ## Smart Tip
> One of the most common cleaning mistakes is to apply a cleaning compound and then start scrubbing or rinsing before the compound has a chance to loosen the dirt or grease. Whenever you apply a cleaning compound, follow the manufacturer's instructions, which will usually tell you to wait 30 seconds or longer before you wipe or scrub.

formulas for concept, name, services offered, etc. That's both an advantage and a drawback. The advantage is that you can do things your way. The drawback is that you have no guidelines to follow. Everything you do, from defining your market to cleaning a bathtub, is a result of trial and error. As an independent owner, you must research every aspect of the business, both before and during your business's lifetime, so you'll start right and adapt to market changes. It's very important to thoroughly investigate any franchise offering before you invest.

Buying an Existing Business

An alternative to starting your own cleaning service business is to take over an existing operation. This may seem like an attractive and simple shortcut to skip over the work involved in building a business from ground zero, but you should approach this option with caution.

You'll find cleaning businesses for sale advertised in trade publications, local newspapers, and through business brokers. The businesses can often be purchased lock, stock, and barrel, including equipment, office supplies, existing accounts—and reputation. Be sure you're getting the quality you're paying for in all aspects.

Of course, there are drawbacks to buying a business. Though the actual dollar amounts depend on the size and type of business, it often takes more cash to buy an existing business than to start one yourself. When you buy a company's assets, you usually get stuck with at least some of the liabilities, as well. And it's highly unlikely that you'll find an existing business that's precisely the company you would have built on your own. Even so, you might find the business you want is currently owned by someone else.

Why do people sell businesses—especially profitable ones? There are a variety of reasons.

Above and Beyond

Regardless of the type of cleaning business you start, you'll probably have the opportunity to do more for your customers than simply clean. Residential cleaning operators regularly alert their clients to potential problems, such as frayed electrical cords and leaky faucets. Commercial cleaners can provide similar observations. In fact, in early 2005 in Montreal, Quebec, a sharp-eyed janitor did more than point out a problem—he saved the life of a 4-year-old boy.

While taking out the garbage at a restaurant, the janitor spotted a car in the normally empty parking lot. He decided to check it out, and when he did, he realized the car was running and saw a plastic tube going from the exhaust pipe into the trunk. The janitor called 911, and when police arrived, they found the boy and his 28-year-old father in the car. The father was in the midst of a bitter divorce and custody battle with the child's mother and was trying to kill himself and his son. Because the janitor was paying attention and took action, both the boy and his father were saved, and the father was charged with attempted murder.

Jani-King International Inc., a commercial cleaning franchisor, now trains its franchisees to assess potential building and workplace security threats and report them to authorities. "Our crews clean the same buildings night after night. We see the normal activity. We want our employees to understand how to spot suspicious activity and then how to report it," says Jerry Crawford, the company's president.

Many entrepreneurs are happiest during the startup and early growth stages of a company; once the business is running smoothly, they get bored and begin looking for something new. Other business owners may grow tired of the responsibility, or be facing health or other personal issues that motivate them to sell their companies. They may be ready to retire and want to turn their hard work into cash for their golden years. In fact, some of the most successful entrepreneurs go into business with a solid plan for how they're going to get out of the business when the time comes.

It's also possible that the business is for sale because it has problems—and while that may not stop you from buying it, you should know all the details before you make a final decision. The following steps will help you:

- *Find out why the business is for sale.* Don't accept what the current owner says at face value; do some research to make an independent confirmation.

- *Examine the business's financial records for the previous three years and for the current year-to-date.* Compare tax records with the owner's claims of revenue and profits.

- *Spend a few days observing the cleaning operation.* Monitor several work crews on the job.

- *Speak with current customers.* Are they satisfied with the service? Are they willing to give a new owner a chance? Ask for their input, both positive and negative, and ask what you can do to improve the operation. Remember, even though sales volume and cash flow may be a primary reason for buying an existing business, customers are under no obligation to stay with you when you take over.

- *Consider hiring someone skilled in business acquisitions.* He or she can assist you in negotiating the sale price and terms of the deal.

- *Remember you can walk away from the deal at any point in the negotiation process—*before a contract is signed.

Beware!
Always use caution when cleaning around computer equipment and electronics, whether you're in a home or an office, especially when you're using chemicals. Never unplug electrical cords, and be careful not to get any liquids on the devices.

Sometimes an owner who is selling a business will stay on after the sale for a time to help the new owner learn the ropes. Depending on the size and complexity of the business and your familiarity with the industry, you may want to negotiate this as part of your purchase contract.

Regardless of whether you start from scratch, buy an existing business, or purchase a franchise, you need a plan. In Chapter 7, we'll talk about how to put that all-important plan together.

Residential Cleaning Service

Housecleaning: It's one of those necessary evils that most people dislike intensely. Even people who don't mind doing housework often find their time budgets stretched thin. The solution? Hire someone to do it. And that "someone" is usually a cleaning service.

Although providing residential cleaning services isn't exactly glamorous, the low startup costs and high sales potential make it attractive to many entrepreneurs. You probably have enough in the way of supplies and equipment in your own home right now to start a residential cleaning service. Another attraction of this business is the hours. A 40-hour workweek is virtually unheard of in the entrepreneurial world, but it's quite realistic with a residential cleaning service. Many operators work Monday through Friday, 8 A.M. to 5 P.M., doing the housecleaning during the day while their clients are at work. And they get to take holidays off because their clients don't want them around on those days.

A residential cleaning service is a great homebased business that you can run by yourself or with employees. As your business grows, you may choose to rent a small office with some storage space, but many successful operators never need to take that step.

Today's typical residential cleaning service has several cleaners on staff, and the owner participates minimally in the cleaning duties, if at all. Owners generally take care of scheduling, handling customer relations issues, ordering supplies, answering the telephone, payroll, and billing, while the cleaners do the actual cleaning. Certainly, there are owners who also clean, but as your business grows, you'll find your time is better spent running the business.

Who Are Your Customers?

Having a maid or housekeeper used to be a symbol of wealth. Only the rich could afford to hire someone to come into their homes to clean. Middle-class women who stayed home while their husbands worked were expected to do their own cleaning. But times have changed. Residential cleaning services no longer cater only to the wealthy. Both middle- and upper-income consumers recognize the value of cleaning services and can afford to hire them.

The primary benefit a residential cleaning service provides is time savings. What would take some customers a whole day, or even an entire weekend, can be handled by a professional cleaner or team of cleaners in just a few hours.

Some customers have the service do all their cleaning; others do light cleaning themselves and depend on their service for heavier, more thorough tasks such as scrubbing floors and toilets, removing cobwebs, and handling other tasks that don't need to be done frequently.

One of the primary reasons behind the tremendous growth in the residential cleaning industry is that more women have joined the work force over the past 40 to 50 years. In families where both the husband and wife work, neither spouse wants to spend their limited leisure time on housework, which makes them great candidates for a cleaning service. Families with both spouses working and whose incomes are $60,000 and up are strong candidates for a cleaning service; households with incomes topping $100,000 are even more likely to hire a service to do their cleaning. Even very wealthy families with high six- or seven-figure incomes who have full-time domestic help will often hire outside professional cleaners to assist their employees.

Of course, two-income families aren't your only prospective customers. You'll also work for affluent families in which the wives aren't employed but prefer to spend their time doing things other than housecleaning, as well as singles who don't have the time or inclination to do their own cleaning, and senior citizens who no longer have the physical stamina to clean their homes.

While some businesses have limited customer bases, residential cleaning services have literally millions of potential customers who either rent or own their homes and live in single-family residences, apartments, and condominiums.

Tracking Time

Some cleaning service owners pay employees by the hour, including travel time; others pay only for cleaning time. In either case, you'll need a way—typically a time sheet—for your employees to record hours worked.

At the top of your time sheets, include a place for the employee's name, employee identification number, and pay period. At the bottom, have a place for the employee and the supervisor to sign and date the form. Set up the middle so your employees can legibly record the time they left the office, the location of each job, the time they arrived, the time they completed each job, travel time, and when they returned to the office at the end of the day. Breaks and lunch periods should also be logged on the time sheet. Use daily time sheets that are turned in at the end of each day rather than weekly logs.

You can use the information you collect on time sheets for more than only payroll. You'll be able to evaluate your scheduling by reviewing the amount of time your crews spend driving. You'll be able to track productivity and address minor problem areas with training before they become major. The information on time sheets also lets you evaluate how accurately you've done your estimates, which means you can determine your profitability before you prepare your monthly financial statements. For a sample employee time sheet, turn to page 34.

Beyond Individual Homes

In addition to occupied homes, you may find a lucrative market cleaning rental homes and apartments between tenants, and in cleaning new homes after the construction crews are finished and before the buyers move in.

Cleaning rental units between tenants requires that you shampoo carpets; scrub floors; clean windows, bathroom, and kitchen fixtures; clean inside and outside of appliances; and wipe down interiors of all cabinets and shelving. Some property managers will also want you to include painting the interior walls as part of your service. You may want to outsource the painting and carpet cleaning.

Builders often have their new homes cleaned when construction is complete. You'll dust; wipe down sinks, tubs and countertops; clean any installation debris from cabinets; wash windows; vacuum; and do other cleaning tasks necessary to get the house ready for occupancy.

One of the biggest appeals of vacant property is that you don't have to navigate around furnishings, and you can usually work fairly quickly. Of course, cleaning rental property that has been abused by the previous tenant can be a particularly unpleasant experience; just wear gloves and, if necessary, a mask, and charge a fair price for the work.

Another opportunity with builders is to clean model homes. Though the homes aren't actually lived in, they sustain a tremendous amount of traffic, and it's critical that they be maintained in sparkling condition, so attention to detail is especially important. Even though they're furnished, model homes don't have the volume of belongings and clutter that occupied dwellings do, and you can generally clean them faster.

Multi-unit residential complexes—either apartments or condos—also need to have their common areas cleaned, such as the laundry rooms, clubhouses, and offices. While this may seem more like a job for a janitorial service, you can present a strong case for using your service if you regularly have crews on the property cleaning the units themselves.

Beware!

Start small. The demand for good cleaning services far outweighs the availability in the marketplace, and you may be tempted to hire too many employees and try to serve too large an area when you first start. A better approach is to limit your geographic market to reduce travel time and expenses when you're starting out.

While each of these markets represents a serious business opportunity, it's important to keep in mind that they're very different from cleaning occupied homes. Some people enjoy this kind of work, and others don't. You'll typically have more of a personal relationship with your customers when you do residential cleaning rather than construction or rental home cleaning, so decide if this is important to you as you plan your business.

Who Are Your Competitors?

Your primary competition will come from other residential cleaning services, both franchises and independents. When you compete with a franchise, you compete with a name that's usually supported by a strong marketing machine. This may seem intimidating, but if you distinguish yourself with superior service and special touches, you'll succeed.

A large competitor won't necessarily compete more intensely than a smaller one. Generally it's the quality of service, rather than the size of the operation, that determines customer satisfaction and leads to referrals.

If your market includes apartment complexes, you may be competing against the cleaning staff of the complex, or against janitorial services that also target this market.

Of course, you're always going to be competing against your own customers. After all, you provide a service that most of your customers could do for themselves. This is important to remember when you're developing your sales strategy. Though your customers may not want to, the reality is that most of them could do for themselves what they're paying you to do for them. Because of this, you need to remind them of the opportunity cost of your service—that is, help them see how much your service is worth to them.

For example, say your customer earns $20 per hour at her job. If she were to clean her own home, it would take her five hours. But if she were working for those five hours, she would have earned $100. As a professional, you can clean her home in less time and for less money—say, in three hours for $75. Now it's up to the customer to determine the opportunity cost of using your service. This is your chance to point out how valuable and limited her time is, and how you can enrich her life by freeing her up to concentrate on her career or participate in leisure activities.

> **Tip...**
>
> **Smart Tip**
> Many customers view their relationships with housecleaners as personal, so they look for a cleaning service that's stable and has been around for a while. Your marketing materials and personal sales efforts should reflect your commitment to the business and longevity in the community.

Equipment

The basic equipment necessary to start a residential cleaning service is the same equipment you use to clean your own home—and chances are, you already own just about everything you need. The essential list includes a vacuum cleaner, mop, broom, dustpan, all-purpose cleaner, glass cleaner, and rags. Even if you have to buy everything new, about $350 to $450 should cover the cost for a one- or two-person operation. Many solo cleaning service operators use their customers' equipment and supplies, so you could probably get started for far less than that.

The only major piece of equipment you'll need is a vehicle. Just about any economical car—including the one you already own—will be adequate. You need one vehicle per crew, or you might allow your cleaners to use their own cars. You may also want your employees to wear uniforms, which allows them to be easily identified and add a degree of professionalism to your operation.

Beyond the items you'll use for cleaning, you'll need some office equipment and furnishings so you can conduct your administrative tasks, and store equipment and supplies.

> **Smart Tip**
>
> Soft-bristle paint brushes are great for dusting louvered doors, vents, and similar surfaces. Soft toothbrushes can get the dust out of furniture that has intricate detail carved in the wood.

Initial Equipment and Supply Checklist

- ❏ Abrasive tile cleanser
- ❏ All-purpose cleaner
- ❏ Brooms
- ❏ Buckets
- ❏ Upright vacuums
- ❏ Canister vacuums
- ❏ City maps/GPS devices
- ❏ Company vehicle
- ❏ Cotton mops
- ❏ Degreaser
- ❏ Dishwashing soap
- ❏ Dust cloths
- ❏ Dust mops
- ❏ Dustpans
- ❏ Extension cords
- ❏ Furniture oil
- ❏ Furniture polish
- ❏ Hand brushes
- ❏ Nonabrasive tile cleanser
- ❏ Paper facemasks
- ❏ Rags
- ❏ Rubber gloves
- ❏ Security system
- ❏ Signage
- ❏ Sponge mops
- ❏ Sponges
- ❏ Spray bottles
- ❏ Stepladders
- ❏ Upright vacuums
- ❏ Window/glass cleaner
- ❏ Wood floor cleaner

The first item you buy will most likely be an industrial vacuum cleaner. Residential vacuum cleaners may do the job, but they're designed for occasional use, not for heavy use on a daily basis. Industrial vacuum cleaners are available in both upright and canister models, and you should buy at least one of each. They generally start between $200 and $300 and up, but they last longer than less expensive units. To prevent vacuums from marking furniture if they bump up against it, place a protective pad around the machine.

You'll need a complete set of equipment and supplies for each of your cleaning crews. Each team should have a cotton mop, sponge mop, dust mop, stepladder, extension cord for each vacuum, and plenty of rags and cleaning cloths. Each team should have one of the following items per person: hand brush, spray bottle of each cleaning solution you use, and a pair of rubber gloves. Two buckets are required for each person conducting wet work—one to hold the cleaning solution, and one to use to wring out your sponge or mop.

It's also a good idea for each crew to have more than one vacuum as a backup, since you can't stop cleaning just because the vacuum cleaner breaks.

Many one-person operations opt to use their customers' supplies and equipment. They charge for labor only, and use the products and tools their customers prefer. One of Fenna Owens' Orlando customers says, "When Fenna told me I needed a new vacuum cleaner, I just asked her what she wanted and bought that."

Supplies

Take a stroll down the cleaning products aisle of your local supermarket, and you may be overwhelmed by the number and variety of products. Many of these items claim to be designed for specialized cleaning tasks. In reality, you need only a handful of cleaning supplies to make a house sparkle—and those supplies don't need to come in fancy packaging, either. Basically, you'll need window cleaner, degreaser, all-purpose cleaner, furniture polish, tile cleanser, wood floor cleaner, paper facemasks, and dust cloths. The more homes you clean in a given day, the more supplies you'll use.

You may find that you need to use additional cleaning chemicals for specific cleaning jobs your customers request. For example, if you service a number of homes with marble, you may want to clean the marble as part of your basic service, and you'll need a special cleaner to do it properly without damaging the surface.

If you offer additional specialty services, such as silverware or brass polishing, you'll need to purchase cleaning solutions for these jobs, as well. If you're unsure about which chemical you need to clean a particular item, ask your customer if they have a preference, or ask a knowledgeable colleague. If they can't help, your local library should have plenty of books on how to clean a variety of different—and even unusual—items. You can also find plenty of help on the internet. For additional advice, you can contact companies that manufacture cleaning products.

For an idea of how much you'll spend on cleaning supplies, see the chart below.

Standard Operations

Before you can set up an operational plan, you need to decide if you'll clean multi-unit dwellings, single-family residences, or a mixture of both. Single-family residences are considered best when you're starting out. They offer more rooms and more square footage. This results in higher revenue than apartments and condominium units, which are typically smaller. As you and your staff gain experience and your efficiency improves, you'll find multi-unit dwellings will become profitable.

What Will You Clean?

Your service will clean the same rooms you usually clean in your own home. A basic cleaning typically includes dusting, vacuuming, cleaning fixtures, mopping floors, wiping counters, and making beds. For an extra charge, some residential cleaning services wash windows, clean carpets, buff floors, wash walls, clean basements, and clean patios and balconies. You may want to establish a list of what you will and won't do, or you may choose to be more flexible. Many cleaning operators use a checklist,

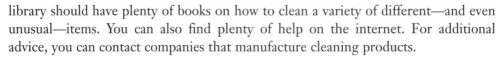

Monthly Supply Costs

The amount you spend on cleaning supplies will vary depending on the size of your operation; the ranges below cover a small, homebased operation up to a very large, commercially based cleaning service.

Abrasive tile cleanser	$20–$325	Nonabrasive tile cleanser	$18–$225
All-purpose cleaner	$38–$600	Paper facemasks	$15–$50
Degreaser	$8–$90	Rags	$25–$75
Dishwashing soap	$10–$75	Sponges	$30–$425
Dust cloths	$25–$175	Window/glass cleaner	$20–$125
Furniture oil	$9–$65	Wood floor cleaner	$15–$85
Furniture polish	$20–$225		

Beware!
Feather dusters are great cleaning tools, but they can also be dangerous. If you're not careful with them, they can knock over and damage delicate figurines. Or, as they begin to wear down, the tips of the feathers can scratch wood surfaces. Use feather dusters with caution.

but Owens says she does "anything that the person who owns the house doesn't like to do."

Most residential cleaning services have a list of tasks that are part of their basic services, plus a list of tasks that they will do for an extra fee. Sometimes your customers will ask you to do things that aren't on either of these lists, such as carpet cleaning, stripping and buffing floors, and exterior window washing.

You can, of course, simply decline some jobs, explaining that you don't offer these services. Or you can subcontract them to reliable companies. If you're going to do this, remember to choose your subcontractors with care, because how well they perform will reflect on you. Or you may choose to rent the necessary equipment and handle the job yourself. If you're asked to do a particular job frequently enough, you may consider purchasing the appropriate equipment and adding it to your list of available extras.

How Will You Clean?

Either an individual or a team can clean a home. Although it naturally takes longer for an individual to do the job, some customers would rather have only one person clean for them. This way, they deal with the same person every time, building a strong, more personal relationship with the cleaner.

Team cleaning allows your firm to operate more efficiently. Customers who are concerned about how much time your cleaners will be in their homes will appreciate the speed of a team. Teams typically consist of two or three people. One approach is to assign each team member certain rooms to clean. Another approach for a two-member team is for one to take care of all the dry work (vacuuming, dusting, making beds, taking out the trash), while the other handles the wet work (mopping, wiping counters, scrubbing bathrooms, and washing dishes). As a way to break the monotony, team members can alternate duties at each home or on a daily or weekly basis.

Encouraging good chemistry between team members is essential. Keep teams together as much as possible; switching crew

Tip...

Smart Tip
Plastic spray bottles work better than aerosol cans because they allow you to spray chemicals more directly; aerosol cans tend to waste cleansers because they release particles into the air as well as on the surface you're cleaning. Also, spray bottles are refillable, and aerosol cans aren't.

On Duty

To clean efficiently, conduct the same cleaning services at each customer's home. As part of their basic service, most residential cleaning services offer the following:

- ○ Dust entire home, including furniture and blinds
- ○ Vacuum entire home, including carpeting and furniture
- ○ Scrub bathtubs and showers
- ○ Clean toilets
- ○ Scrub sinks and faucets
- ○ Clean kitchen and bathroom countertops
- ○ Clean outside of appliances
- ○ Wipe down inside of microwave oven
- ○ Wipe down outside of kitchen cupboards
- ○ Make beds
- ○ Polish furniture
- ○ Collect and dispose of trash
- ○ Clean mirrors
- ○ Wipe television screens

In addition to these basic tasks, you may offer additional services for an extra charge. Those services may include:

- ○ Change bed and bath linens
- ○ Clean inside of refrigerator
- ○ Defrost freezer
- ○ Clean oven and underneath stovetop
- ○ Wash walls
- ○ Clean out fireplace
- ○ Strip, wax, and buff floors
- ○ Oil woodwork
- ○ Clean carpets
- ○ Wash windows
- ○ Wipe windowsills, baseboards, doors, and door frames

members from one team to another tends to destabilize all the teams. Make changes within teams only when a crew member is promoted to supervisor, when a member requests a transfer, or when a personality conflict arises.

If a crew member isn't getting along with his or her teammates and team morale and productivity seem to be affected because of it, transfer the crew member to another team. But do such a transfer only once. If that person doesn't get along with the new teammates, it's probably time to let him or her go.

You may want to designate one member of the team as the team leader or supervisor. Usually, that person has the most experience with your company and knows all your policies and procedures. If you have a large enough staff, you may want a supervisor to oversee several teams. Typically, supervisors assign duties to team members, hold customers' keys, and drive team members to each home. The best approach is to promote from within after someone has demonstrated that they're responsible and trustworthy and will represent the company in a positive manner.

Scheduling

It's important to schedule your work in a way that keeps travel time between jobs to a minimum. For example, if you have two or more customers in an apartment or condominium complex, clean them on the same day. The same advice applies to single-family homes; schedule clients who are close together or in the same neighborhood on the same day. You can schedule the home closest to your office (or wherever the cleaners are starting from) first, and proceed in order to the home furthest away, or vice versa. Always account for both cleaning time and travel time when you establish your work schedules.

Owens says when she first started her Florida business, her clients were spread all over the greater Orlando area. It didn't take her long to realize she was spending almost as much time traveling between jobs as she was cleaning. So she restructured her schedule based on her clients' geographic locations and is now far more productive.

The ideal travel time is no more than 15 to 20 minutes between each client. Volume is the name of the game in this business. The more time you spend cleaning and the less time you spend traveling, the more you'll earn.

A two-person cleaning team can usually clean an apartment in about an hour. The same team may take between one and two hours to clean a moderately sized house. This team could reasonably be expected to clean seven individual apartments in the same complex in one day, or as many as four or five houses, if travel time isn't excessive.

What Does a Typical Day Include?

The day should begin with each crew checking its equipment to make sure team members have everything they need and that there's enough of each cleaning solution

Bright Idea

If your employees drive their own cars to jobs, invest in magnetic signs that they can place on their vehicles to promote your company. The signs can be easily removed when employees aren't working and they cost far less than painting a car.

to last the entire day. They should gather whatever paperwork they need and then head to their first job.

Each crew should fill out a checklist of routine cleaning duties on each job, which is then placed in the customer's file (see page 35 for a sample checklist). The checklist includes a space for the date of the service and the initials of the individual who performs each duty. This serves as a reminder to the cleaners so they don't accidentally forget to do something, and it gives you a way to follow up with the appropriate person if the customer complains about the quality of the work.

Your cleaners should clean according to a system. Most people cleaning their homes waste time retracing their steps because they don't use a systematic plan. They miss things, forget what they've cleaned, and keep running back to the kitchen for sponges or sprays. Certainly allow your crews some flexibility in how they operate, but be sure they're cleaning in the most efficient, logical way. Clockwise from the top of the house is a good method to use.

At the end of the day, crews should turn in their paperwork, replenish their supplies, and advise their supervisor of anything that occurred during the day that might need attention.

From That First Phone Call

When a prospective customer calls, be friendly and knowledgeable about all the services you offer. Be prepared to explain your pricing policy, the services included in a basic cleaning, and when you expect payment. Keep customer information forms close to your telephone so you can write down the information as you get it. The form will also serve as a guide for you so you're sure to ask for all the necessary information.

You may give your estimates over the phone or in person (see Chapter 9 for an explanation of how to set your prices). Estimating over the phone saves you the time of traveling and walking through the prospect's home. On the other hand, when you can't see the home, you don't know its true condition—your crew may get

Smart Tip

Tip...

You may want to charge extra for the first cleaning, especially if the home hasn't been professionally cleaned in a long time. You can justify an additional fee because you'll likely spend more time on your initial visit.

there and find that it's extremely dirty and has a lot of items lying around that need to be moved and cleaned.

Whether you make your quote over the phone or in person, you need to know how many square feet the home is, what tasks the customer wants done, how many bedrooms there are and how many beds each has, the number of bathrooms, the number of people who reside in the home, the number of children, the number and type of pets, whether there's an alarm system, and where your staff can obtain a key if the owner won't be home when the crew arrives. You'll need to know if there are any expensive items in the house, such as figurines and artwork. If there are a lot of

Pay Day

Many residential cleaning services expect payment either before or at the time of cleaning. This isn't unusual, and most customers are used to this type of arrangement and won't object to it. Some services are more flexible and will arrange other payment terms.

If your policy is payment in advance or at the time of cleaning, decide what you will do if your crew arrives at the home and the customer hasn't left a check. You may want to clean the home anyway and leave a reminder notice for the customer to mail a check. Or you may not clean that day. Sometimes this is a judgment call you'll make based on the customer, how long they've been with you, and how confident you are of payment.

If you decide to not clean a home because the customer failed to pay, you also need to have a policy on paying your cleaners. Some services simply tell their employees to move on to the next job, and they're only paid for what they actually do. If they don't get a full day's work in, they only receive a partial day's wages.

Orlando cleaning service operator Wanda Guzman says dealing with the payment issue is one reason she likes being small enough to know her customers. "If someone forgets to leave a check, I don't worry about it," she says. "My longtime customers do that once in a while, and they always remember the next time. If it's a relatively new customer, I might leave a note or call them." Most of Guzman's established customers pay by the month, even though she cleans every week for them. You may want to check out one of the mobile apps that will allow you to accept payments through your phone or accept payments on your website.

If customers are consistently late with payment or fail to pay on a regular basis, you may want to drop them.

knickknacks, this can affect your price, because moving and dusting them takes time.

Although walk-through estimates take more time, they give you a chance to meet the customer, calculate more accurately how long it will take you to clean the home, and present your company in a favorable light. During the walk-through, look for evidence of pets and children, as well as noting breakable items and small items, such as collectibles and figurines. Ask if there's anything that shouldn't be touched or needs any sort of special handling. If the customer has pets, ask that they be kept in cages, a closed room, or outside in a locked area so they won't interfere with your staff's work and safety. Make a note of the animal's name so your cleaners can use it if the animal should become disagreeable or disappear. Ask about the pet's favorite hangouts so you can pay special attention to cleaning those areas. You should also show the customer evidence of bonding, liability, and workers' compensation insurance.

> **Bright Idea**
>
> Provide your customers with a list of the cleaning products you'll be using in their homes and ask them to let you know if they have any allergies to chemicals or if there are any products they would prefer you not use.

At the end of your walk-through, calculate your estimate and give the price to the customer. If the customer agrees to the fee, complete a customer agreement form that you both sign and both keep a copy of, and put the customer on your cleaning schedule. Obtain a key to the customer's home, and, if there's an alarm system, get the code and special instructions your crew will need to avoid setting off the alarm.

Keep in mind that the first time you clean a customer's home will usually take longer than your subsequent visits. The home might need a thorough cleaning before you can shift to regularly scheduled maintenance cleaning, and you may want to send extra crew members in for that first visit.

Maintaining Customer Records

Keep a file on each prospective customer that includes their name, address, size of home, services inquired about, the quote you gave, and the results of your sales contact. If they didn't hire you, you should find out why. If you're consistently losing jobs because your prices are high, you may want to think about restructuring your pricing or operation to make yourself more competitive. If the problem was that you couldn't meet the prospect's schedule—for example, if they want you to clean on a day that you don't have any crews in the area—make a note and follow up in a few months to see if their needs have changed.

Once someone agrees to use your service, set up a customer file. Even if it is only a one-time visit, you may be able to turn that visit into a regular contract with proper follow-up.

Your customer file should include a customer information sheet (see sample on page 36) that includes:

- Customer's name
- Spouse's name
- Address
- All telephone numbers (home, work, cell)
- Email address
- Contact person, in case the customer is unavailable
- Number of bedrooms
- Number of bathrooms
- Total square footage of home
- Type of residence (apartment, condo, townhouse, house)
- Number and ages of children
- Number and type of pets
- If pets are kept indoors or outdoors
- If the home has an alarm system

Additional information you want to gather is up to you. You may also want to note on your customer information sheet the cost estimate and service description you provided.

When customers agree to use your service, it's a good idea to have them sign agreements that clearly state how often your cleaners will visit, how much each visit will cost, which cleaning services you'll provide during each visit, when payment is due, and your cancellation policy. A signed contract will prevent future misunderstandings. Keep it in the customer's file.

You should also file the completed checklists that cover all the duties the cleaners need to perform with each cleaning in the customer's file. If the customer complains that the bed wasn't made or the kitchen floor wasn't cleaned properly, you can refer to the checklist to see who was responsible for the particular task. If there's ever any damage to a customer's property, you'll want to complete a damage report (see sample on page 37) and maintain it in the customer's file.

> **Bright Idea**
>
> Be willing to make your sales calls and do your estimates in the evenings and on weekends. Although most of the work involved in running a residential cleaning service is done during normal business hours, you may need to make your initial visits to customers' homes at times convenient to them so they don't have to take time off work.

Additional documents that you'll keep in a customer's file include cleaning schedules, billing sheets, and any correspondence or special notes you may make about the customer.

Pitfalls

As with any business, there are certain pitfalls that go along with running a cleaning service. No matter what you do, some customers will never be satisfied. These customers typically want absolutely everything cleaned but also want the lowest price.

To handle problem customers, start by recognizing and addressing their concerns. While you shouldn't admit to a mistake until you're sure you're at fault, always recognize the validity of the customer's feelings. Say something like "I can certainly understand why this is an important issue for you. I need to get a little more information before I can take the appropriate action."

Ask them what aspects of the service they're dissatisfied with and what needs to be improved. If the problem is with the quality of service, discuss the situation with the employees responsible for cleaning that customer's home. Take the time to visit the customer's home before and after your crew cleans.

> **Smart Tip**
> Always discuss customer concerns and complaints with the employees responsible for the work. If the concern is valid, address the issue by training the employees. If it's not, go back to the customer and clear up the communication problem.

If, after doing this, the customer still feels they aren't receiving their money's worth, but your crew members are doing their jobs properly, explain what your basic services cover and give your customer the option of paying a higher price for additional service. If they're not willing to pay more but are still demanding more, it may be better to drop the customer rather than dealing with complaints after every cleaning.

Another pitfall facing cleaning service owners is that some customers may take a haughty attitude with the cleaners, which can have an impact on your employees' morale. While it's a fact that cleaning homes isn't the most prestigious or financially rewarding line of work, that's no reason for your customers to treat your employees poorly. Cleaning is an honest and necessary job, and your employees deserve to be treated with respect. If you become aware that a customer isn't treating your cleaners with respect, have a tactful conversation with the customer, pointing out that your employees come from good backgrounds, are trustworthy and well trained, and are providing a valuable service that your customer probably doesn't want to do without. This is usually sufficient to correct the situation, but if the customer continues to adopt an attitude that distresses your employees, you may want to consider dropping the account.

In several parts of the country, many cleaning service employees are recent immigrants who may have a difficult time assimilating and communicating. Consider working with local community resources that offer an English as a Second Language class so these employees can learn to communicate better with other employees and customers. Keep in mind that they won't adjust to American culture and to using English overnight. Give them time, and work with them. But if they don't seem to be making sufficient effort or progress, and their work—and consequently your business—suffers as a result, you may not be able to afford to keep them on.

One of the challenges of owning a residential cleaning service is scheduling around holidays. Most of your customers will prefer that their cleaning be done when they're not home, and they certainly won't want you around during their holiday parties. So if a client's regular cleaning day is Monday, you need a plan for how you're going to

---

Security Is the Key

The majority of your customers won't be home when you or your employees clean their homes, so you need to arrange for access to the premises. Some residential cleaning services require the customer to provide a key to the house or the code to a keyless entry system.

Others are more flexible. Because some customers are reluctant to hand over their keys, some cleaning service operators are willing to pick up a key from a neighbor, from the mailbox, or from some outside hiding place. This isn't a great idea, because an absent-minded customer can disrupt your work schedule by forgetting to leave the key in the agreed-on spot. Or the neighbor who has the key may not be home when your crew arrives. And, leaving a key outside is a security risk for your customer. The easiest, most efficient policy is to have a key or some other form of assured access to the residence.

For both your own and your customers' protection, create a security system for the keys. Tag each key with a code that doesn't identify your customer or their address. The corresponding identification information for the code should be kept in a location separate from the keys, ideally in a password-protected computer file or in a locked safe. Keep the keys in another safe or locked key box. To increase your customers' peace of mind, explain your key security system to them.

If a key is lost or stolen while in your possession, notify the customer immediately and offer to pay the cost of rekeying the locks.

handle all the holidays that fall on Mondays, such as Presidents' Day, Memorial Day, and Labor Day. If the regular cleaning day is Thursday, know how you'll handle Thanksgiving. Be sensitive to ethnic and religious holidays that you may not celebrate but your clients do—and consider how you'll handle things if the situation is reversed and you're observing holidays

Smart Tip

Test every surface before using a new cleaning solution. Be sure the solution won't remove color or mar the finish.

your clients don't. Check the calendar at the beginning of the year to see what day other major holidays fall on and put together a plan for how you're going to handle every holiday and vacation.

Some of your weekly customers won't mind if you just skip them once. Others will prefer that you reschedule for the day before or after the holiday. It's a juggling act that can test every bit of your managerial talent, so plan for holidays well in advance by discussing the schedule with your customers and employees.

In addition to regular cleaning, you may want to offer your customers special services—such as a spring cleaning—once or twice a year, where you do such extras as cleaning the inside of cabinets, help with closet cleaning and organizing, and even help with cleaning out the garage, attic, or basement. Your customers may be comfortable telling you what they want and leaving you to do the job, or they may want to work with you to direct the sorting and organizing. In the latter case, they may prefer to schedule these projects on weekends, which means overtime for you and your crew.

Oops!

Accidents happen, so from time to time, damage to a customer's property may occur. Most customers are reasonable when these things happen, especially if you immediately accept your responsibility to repair or replace the item. If the damage is minor, you'll probably want to just absorb the cost of the repair; if it's major, you'll file a claim with your insurance company.

You should have a procedure in place to deal with damage incidents. Begin with a report form that the responsible employee should fill out and turn in to his or her supervisor, or to you. The form should include the employee's name, the date of the incident, the customer, the item involved, the value of the item, a full description of how the damage or breakage occurred, and what follow-up actions took place (see the Damage Report form on page 37). Take several photos from various angles that clearly show the affected item or area.

For minor damage, you may just leave your customer a note explaining what happened and outlining what you intend to do to rectify the situation. For a more serious incident, call the customer immediately to discuss the best way to handle it.

Cleaning for a Reason

Deborah Sardone, president and CEO of Buckets & Bows Maid Service Inc. in Lewisville, Texas, has been touched by both clients and employees who have experienced the devastating impact of cancer. In 2006, she formed the Cleaning for a Reason Foundation to provide free professional housecleaning services for women who are undergoing cancer treatment. In dealing with a cancer diagnosis, the patient and caregivers tend to focus primarily on medical issues; basic lifestyle matters are often overlooked. Yet a clean environment, while always important, is especially valuable to cancer patients, and many of them don't have the financial resources to pay for professional cleaning. Hundreds of cleaning services across the country partner with the foundation to clean the homes of women who are struggling with the debilitating effects of cancer and chemotherapy—doing it at no charge as a way of helping others and giving back to their communities.

To learn more about the foundation and how your cleaning service can participate, visit cleaningforareason.org.

Always offer to arrange for the repair yourself; never suggest that your customer do it and just tell you how much it cost. Remember, the primary benefit of using a cleaning service is saving time, and your customers will probably not be happy about having to spend their time replacing or repairing a broken item. Of course, if they offer to do it, it's OK to agree.

In addition to making the customer happy, you'll also want to find out if the damage was a genuine accident or if the employee was careless. You may want to implement a policy in which all or part of the cost (up to the amount of your insurance deductible, of course) of replacing or repairing damaged items is deducted from the responsible person's pay; this reduces your expenses and keeps employees on their toes.

Whether or not you file a claim with your insurance company depends, of course, on the amount of the claim and the type of coverage you have.

Make it clear to your employees that all incidents of damage, no matter how minor they may appear, must be reported, and that failing to do so could result in disciplinary action up to and including termination.

▲

Employee Time Sheet

Name: _____

Social Security number: _____

Date: _____

Time left office: _____

Customer (Include address and phone number)	Time Arrived	Time Completed

Time returned to office: _____

Employee signature: _____ Date: _____

Supervisor signature: _____ Date: _____

Checklist of Routine Cleaning Duties

Duty	Date	Initials
Restrooms		
Empty trash		
Dust light fixtures		
Dust counters		
Wipe mirrors		
Clean sink		
Wipe countertops		
Wipe cabinets		
Clean tub/shower/toilet		
Bedrooms and/or Living Room, Study, etc.		
Empty trash		
Make beds		
Dust furniture		
Dust miniblinds		
Vacuum drapes		
Vacuum floor and under bed		
Kitchen		
Dust tops of cabinets		
Wipe tops and front of appliances		
Wipe cabinets		
Clean sink		
Clean countertops		
Sweep floors		
Mop floors		
General Cleaning		
Empty trash		
Clean windows		
Wipe windowsills		
Remove cobwebs		
Clean light switches		
Wipe walls		
Wipe door handles and frames		
Wipe telephones		
Dust miniblinds		
Dust furniture		
Polish furniture		
Clean mirrors		
Sweep floors		

Customer Information Sheet

Name: _____ Spouse's name: _____

Address: _____

Home phone: _____ Work phone: _____

Cell phone: _____ Email: _____

Number to call in case of emergency: _____

Type of facility: House ❏   Apartment/Condo ❏   Townhouse ❏

Square footage: _____

Number of bedrooms: _____

Number of bathrooms: _____

Number of children: _____ Ages: _____

Number of pets: _____ Types: _____ Indoors/Outdoors

Does home have security system? _____ Code: _____

Date received customer's key: _____

Additional comments: _____

_____

_____

_____

_____

_____

_____

_____

_____

_____

_____

_____

_____

Damage Report

Date: _____

Customer name: _____

Address: _____

Home phone: _____ Work phone: _____

Staff person responsible: _____

Item(s) description: _____

_____

_____

_____

_____

Replacement value of item(s): _____

_____

Please describe the incident that caused the damage: _____

_____

Was damage documented by photo or video? _____

Can item be repaired? _____

Was customer notified? _____

By whom? _____

Date and time: _____

Please describe follow-up procedure (i.e., item repaired or replaced):

_____

_____

_____

_____

Cost: _____

_____

Was insurance company notified? _____

_____

Date of notification: _____

_____

4

Janitorial Service

Look around. Just about any place where you see a commercial facility, you're looking at a cleaning opportunity. While residential cleaning services typically only clean residences, janitorial services clean businesses—offices, hospitals, restaurants, and schools, to name a few. And what a janitorial service lacks in glamour it makes up for in potential profits.

he demand for janitorial services is strong and will likely continue to be. It just
s sense that as long as there are commercial buildings, there will always be a need
omeone to clean them. Even during recessions, janitorial businesses do well.

While it typically takes more than a residential cleaning service, the startup costs
for a janitorial business are still relatively low. It's possible to get started working from
a homebased office with just a vehicle and a minimal amount of equipment.

But while residential services are pretty much "normal business hours" operations,
janitorial services are almost the opposite. You'll find some customers who want you
to clean during the day, but most will prefer that you clean after their staff has finished
their work and gone home.

With few exceptions, janitorial jobs are going to be substantially larger than residential cleaning ones—even if you start with very small customers. "If you took someone who was used to cleaning homes and put them in a large office building, they
would hesitate and think they couldn't do that huge space," says Michael W. Ray,
owner of Pro Building Services Inc., a janitorial service in Salt Lake City. The key is
to not be intimidated; just break the work down into tasks that can be done in a logical, reasonable order.

Who Are Your Customers?

Though not all businesses will hire an outside janitorial service company, their
facilities all need to be cleaned. Not only must they meet health code requirements,
but they also want to make a favorable impression on their customers. Offices and
office buildings are the primary customers of most janitorial services, but you can also
do well cleaning restaurants, schools (including colleges and universities), hospitals,
medical offices, museums, retail stores, ware-
houses, and manufacturing facilities.

Many janitorial companies begin by cleaning
small offices. The work involves dusting, vacuuming, removing trash, and cleaning restrooms
and lunchrooms. When you're ready, you can
expand your services to include cleaning windows, buffing floors, and shampooing carpets.

After you get some experience with small
offices, you can move up to larger facilities and
other types of businesses.

What and how you clean depends on the
customer and their type of business. For example, when you clean medical facilities, you'll be

> **Bright Idea**
>
> Consider backpack-
> style vacuum cleaners.
> Michael Ray says his Salt Lake
> City employees can vacuum
> three to five times the amount
> of space in the same time
> with a backpack vacuum as
> they can with a standard
> upright. Good backpack vac-
> uum cleaners run about $250
> to $450 and higher.

cleaning the general office, public areas, and the examination rooms. You need to be aware of blood-borne pathogens, which are microorganisms that are present in human blood and can cause disease in humans, such as hepatitis B virus (HBV) and HIV. Take preventive measures to protect yourself and your employees. When handling any waste that may have been contaminated with blood, always wear latex gloves to reduce the risk of coming in contact with blood-borne pathogens.

You might consider targeting the food-service industry. A growing number of restaurateurs are choosing to hire janitorial services rather than have their own employees clean their facilities. You'll need to go in after the restaurant closes, and clean the waiting area, dining rooms, restrooms, and sometimes the kitchen. You'll vacuum, mop, and clean all glass and light fixtures. If you're responsible for the kitchen, you'll need to clean the grill, other cooking surfaces, and appliances.

Who Are Your Competitors?

Because janitorial services don't require a lot of cash or experience to start, this is a relatively simple business to enter. For the same reason, it's also a competitive one. But if you clean well and provide exceptional customer service, you'll succeed.

Of course, you'll be competing against other janitorial services that range from independent, mom-and-pop operations to large corporations. To compete effectively, it helps to understand how these companies are structured and run. In fact, you'll probably see a description of the company you want to build here.

Often, people will start a janitorial service with every intention of staying small, just to provide a way for couples and families to work together as they service accounts and earn a living. Sometimes the couples are middle-aged, or retired from their first careers. They may have only a few accounts, do the cleaning themselves, and don't need any employees. By working from home and using general cleaning equipment rather than the industrial-quality variety, they keep their overhead low. However, these companies are often so small they can't afford to buy insurance, which means they aren't protected if something happens to their equipment or vehicle, or if they cause—or are injured in—an on-the-job accident. A janitorial service that's adequately insured and bonded has a competitive edge over one that isn't.

Large commercial cleaning companies and franchised operations generally have a name recognition you may find intimidating. They're probably well insured and have top-of-the-line equipment and a sophisticated marketing plan. The real question is, How good is their service? One of the industry's biggest problems is employee turnover, and the more employees a company has, the harder it is to monitor their performance and ensure that the work is being performed satisfactorily. To compete with a large operation, emphasize in your marketing materials that you provide top-quality, personal service, and that your employees are carefully supervised.

Suck It Up

The issue of indoor air quality makes choosing the right vacuum cleaner increasingly important for janitorial services. It's not enough to make the carpet look good; you must consider what the vacuum actually traps and what it allows to escape in the way of particles. Here are some points to consider when shopping for a vacuum cleaner:

○ *Efficient filters*. Filters play a critical role in preventing dust and soil particles from being redistributed into the air. Your best choices are HEPA or HEPA-type filters and machines that feature air-filtering processes that trap and hold dust, soil, allergens, and breathable particles.

○ *Aggressive pile lifting and grooming*. This opens the carpet to allow for more efficient removal of dry soil, dust, and debris. If the vacuum cleaner does this, you can eliminate the need to lift the pile as a separate step, which reduces labor costs.

○ *Strong, consistent airflow*. A powerful airstream will draw more dry soil out of carpet and carry it through the machine into the vacuum bag.

○ *Airtight collector*. Whatever container collects the soil should hold the soil and not release it back out into the air to settle on the building's contents and be inhaled by building occupants.

Salt Lake City's Michael Ray says that when he takes over a building and begins vacuuming with quality equipment, there's a noticeable drop in the dust level within the first 30 days.

You'll also be competing against in-house cleaning staffs. If a company you contact already has in-house custodians, don't discount that company as a potential account. Stress your quality of service and point out that using your company is more cost-effective than maintaining an in-house staff. Many companies today are outsourcing as much as they can, and your sales efforts should put you in an ideal position to win the account if and when the company decides to restructure how they handle cleaning.

Equipment

Though it's not ideal, it's possible to start a janitorial service with as little as a mop, bucket, broom, vacuum cleaner, rags, and some all-purpose cleaner. As you grow, you'll be able to purchase other equipment, such as a floor buffer, a carpet cleaning machine, and better-quality vacuums.

To avoid spending your limited capital on equipment you won't use very often, especially in the beginning, consider renting machines as you need them. Another option is to subcontract jobs requiring special equipment to companies that focus on that type of work, such as carpet cleaning and window washing.

For most janitorial jobs, you'll need a mop, mop bucket and wringer, push broom, baseboard brush, straw broom, pail, scrub brush, squeegee, 6-foot ladder, upright vacuum cleaner, three-prong adapter (to be sure you have power for your electrical equipment), hand scrubbing pads, dustpan, spray bottles, extension ladder, heavy-duty extension cords in either 50- or 75-foot lengths, wax applicator, wheeled trash can, and floor scraper/putty knife.

Floor Cleaning Equipment

In addition to regular vacuuming, janitorial services are often expected to clean floors, which means you may need your own special equipment. To make the best decision on a carpet cleaner, see the equipment section in Chapter 5.

Initial Equipment and Supply Checklist

- All-purpose cleaning powders
- All-purpose cleaning solutions
- Brooms
- Brushes
- Buffing machine pads
- Carpet cleaning machine
- Cleaning carts
- Company vehicle(s)
- Dust cloths
- Dustpans
- Extension cords
- Extension ladder
- Feather dusters
- Floor cleaning machine
- Floor scraper/putty knife
- Floor signs
- Glass cleaner
- Hand scrubbing pads
- Ladder
- Metal storage cabinet
- Mop bucket and wringer
- Mops
- Pumice sticks
- Security system
- Signage
- Soap
- Sponges/pails
- Spray bottles
- Squeegees
- Three-pronged adapters
- Upright vacuum
- Wax applicators
- Wet/dry vacuum
- Wheeled trash cans

You may also want to buy a floor buffer to wax and shine vinyl and tile floors. This machine also strips wax build-up before applying another coat of wax. A basic buffer operates at a speed of 175 to 1,500 RPM. A burnisher is a kind of floor buffer but operates at 1,000 RPM and higher. A new, low-speed floor buffer costs $475 to $1,200, and a burnisher costs $800 to $2,000. If your accounts have a lot of floor space that needs to be shined, a burnisher might be worth the investment. But if you only have a few accounts with uncarpeted floors, a basic buffer will be sufficient.

Chemicals

Most of the cleaning products you'll use aren't dangerous, but you still need to be concerned with issues such as chemical composition, proper storage and use, and environmental friendliness.

"We try to use products that are as safe as possible and yet still effective for the job we need them to do," says Ray. "The strongest chemicals we have are spotters for carpet. Strippers for floor wax are also pretty strong, and so are toilet bowl acids." Some tasks require more powerful compounds than others, and it's important that every worker using dangerous products understand how to use them properly and with as little risk of harm to themselves, the materials being cleaned, and the environment as possible.

Follow the manufacturer's instructions for storage and use. Be sure to provide your employees with proper safety equipment, such as eyeglasses or goggles to shield against chemical splashes, and gloves to protect their hands when they're doing wet work.

Standard Operations

If you like a steady, dependable routine, don't start a janitorial service. Owners in this business can never predict when their days will start or what hours they'll work.

Typically, though, you'll probably start about 9 A.M. Your first order of business will likely be answering customer complaints and questions regarding work your employees did the night before. Clients might complain that carpets weren't properly vacuumed, windows weren't cleaned, restrooms weren't scrubbed, or paper towel dispensers weren't filled. If the complaint is minor and can wait, have the crew supervisor or other designated employee in charge of that account take care of the problem on the next visit. If the

> **Smart Tip** Tip...
> Keep a good backup file of temps you can call on short notice either to substitute for a sick or vacationing employee or as a permanent replacement if necessary.

problem warrants immediate attention, visit the account personally the day you receive the complaint and correct the problem.

The next order of business will be to make customer service calls. Just because customers aren't complaining doesn't mean they're totally satisfied. You should be calling your customers regularly—ideally at least once a week—to make sure they're happy and that there are no areas where you could improve your service.

With your existing customers properly attended to, it's time to get out of the office and call on potential accounts. As your business grows, you may eventually hire a full-time salesperson to handle this aspect of your business, but in the beginning, you'll need to make sales calls yourself.

The cleaning work typically begins in the late afternoon or early evening. Depending on the size of your operation and the number of people on your staff, you may or may not be involved in the actual cleaning work, but it's still a good idea for you to be visible when crews begin their shifts.

The typical janitorial service that cleans offices begins cleaning after the office employees have left for the day. If the office closes at 5 P.M., you may be able to begin

Tip...

Smart Tip

When cleaning restrooms, clean for health first and appearance second. Protect public health by minimizing germs, disease-causing microbes, and bacteria. Use clean tools and products appropriate for the specific cleaning job.

Night and Day

Though most janitorial work is performed at night after employees have gone home for the day, there will be times when you'll need to supply workers during the day. A large office building may want you to have a custodian around during the day to maintain the restrooms and clean up unexpected spills. You may want to charge a slightly higher labor rate for this person than you do for your night workers, and be sure you choose someone who not only cleans well but also has good people skills.

Restaurants that cater to lunch and dinner crowds may prefer that you clean in the morning, rather than after closing. Customers that operate 24 hours a day will probably want you to clean during their slowest periods, which will vary depending on the type of business. Never assume the hours your customers want you to work; always ask to be sure.

That's a Lot of Elbow Grease

Square feet cleaned per hour by one FTE, based on interior building area with medium obstructions:

Type of Building	Average	Low	High
School (K-12)	3,047	2,737	3,358
College/university	2,924	2,510	3,338
Industrial plant or warehouse	3,212	2,468	3,957
Hospital	2,473	1,715	3,230
Nursing home	1,192	896	1,488
Private office building	3,127	2,304	3,949
Government facility	3,494	2,630	4,359
Other	2,783	2,060	3,505

Source: Cleaning & Maintenance Management *magazine*

cleaning as early as 6 P.M. But most clients don't want you to begin cleaning until after all the employees have left the building, and if they tend to work late, you may not be able to enter the building until 9 P.M. or later. Some clients will want you to clean daily, others every other day, and still others may only need you to come once a week.

Typically, your employees will be divided into crews of two to six, including a supervisor. The team's supervisor should be someone who knows the job and cleans well, has been with the company a while (usually, but not always, longer than others on the team), and can represent your company well. Supervisors or crew chiefs generally earn one to two dollars more per hour than other team members.

Setting up teams not only speeds the cleaning process but improves efficiency, boosts morale, and promotes honesty. Teams are essential when cleaning large accounts because there's so much work to do, and one person can't handle it alone.

Teams should remain intact from job to job. Moving crew members from team to team is destabilizing. If a team is effective and all the workers get along well, keep them productive by not switching them around unless you really need to.

In general, team members share the responsibility of cleaning a facility with the supervisor. Divide them into two groups: one doing wet work and the other doing dry work.

Smart Tip

Tip...

When you're cleaning, keep moving forward. Plan your work so everything gets done on the first pass through any given space.

Wet work consists of scrubbing or mopping floors and counters, washing walls, cleaning sinks and toilets, and other tasks that involve water. Dry work is virtually everything else, from dusting to vacuuming to polishing floors. If specific team members prefer doing a certain type of work or are better at some tasks than others, accommodate them as much as possible. They'll be happier, and boosting morale means boosting your bottom line.

Bright Idea

If a prospective customer is considering changing to your company from another service, find out why. If you know exactly what they weren't satisfied with, you can pay more attention to those concerns.

Team members should also assist in maintaining equipment, which includes helping the supervisor clean the equipment at the end of each day (or, more likely, night). This is a chore that can be rotated among crew members. Be sure they understand that they're responsible for immediately reporting to the supervisor any problems they have with equipment, either when they're using it or cleaning it, or any other type of on-the-job problems.

In addition to your daily routine, you'll need to plan and carry out a number of weekly and monthly procedures. It's a good idea to maintain a quarterly master plan so you don't forget anything and you properly schedule your time and your staffing.

A Little Help

When a customer asks you to handle a chore that's not part of your normal service, you can do one of three things. One, you can explain that you don't do that and risk damaging your relationship with the customer by forcing him to find another resource. Two, you can agree to do it, then scramble for the necessary equipment and skills to handle the job, and hope you're pricing it reasonably. Or three, you can hire an independent contractor who specializes in that type of work.

Subcontracting special janitorial jobs can save you money on payroll and keep your equipment investment down. For example, you might want to subcontract your carpet cleaning work to a carpet cleaning company, or window washing to a window washer. Other services janitorial customers might occasionally need include ceiling cleaning, sandblasting, and pressure washing.

You would typically use an independent contractor for jobs that only a few of your clients request and that don't need to be performed often.

Like any other business owner, you have to maintain your records and take care of administrative tasks. If you can't find the time during the week, you'll have to devote a few hours on weekends—but whatever you do, you must keep your financial records, including payroll and taxes, current and accurate. To make good operating decisions, you must know where your business is headed at all times. If you neglect these nuts-and-bolts tasks, your entire operation will suffer, no matter how high your sales are.

Laundry

Unless you plan to operate a small, part-time janitorial service, you'll need your own laundry facility. "We use fresh laundry every day," says Ray. That includes rags, towels and mop heads. He maintains an industrial-capacity washer and dryer in his office.

If you're small, your washer and dryer at home may be able to handle your laundry load, or you might choose to use a commercial coin-operated laundry. What's important is that you accurately estimate your laundry needs and are able to meet them. Remember, using dirty equipment won't produce the quality results you've promised and your customers demand.

Maintaining Customer Records

Keep a file on each customer. It should include a schedule of the cleaning duties you perform for them. For example:

- *Daily*. Empty trash, clean restrooms, and restock paper products.
- *Every other day*. Clean windows, vacuum, and dust desks.
- *Weekly*. Mop floors.
- *Monthly*. Dust atificial plants and clean light fixtures.
- *Quarterly*. Clean carpets and dust corners and tops of shelves.

Consider writing dates next to each of these duties so you know just when a certain task needs to be done and when it's actually performed. You may even want to give a copy of this schedule to your customers so they know just what you do and when you do it.

Bidding

When you sell your janitorial services, for the most part, you'll be dealing with experienced businesspeople who prefer to work with professional suppliers. You'll probably be asked to submit a written bid outlining the services you'll perform and the prices you'll charge.

Task Times

Time it takes one FTE to complete cleaning tasks, based on 1,000 square feet of unobstructed floor:

	Average	Low	High
Wet mopping	20.6 minutes	18.9	22.3
Vacuuming	18.2 minutes	16.7	19.8
Dust mopping	12.2 minutes	10.8	13.7

Source: Cleaning & Maintenance Management *magazine*

Use the "Estimate Form" on page 57 to determine what services the customer wants performed and to calculate how much to charge for the job. After you've come up with an estimate, present it formally to the customer in the form of a proposal (see page 58).

Most businesspeople are reasonable and understand that you get what you pay for. Certainly they want to get the lowest price possible—just as you do on the goods and services you have to buy for your own company. But they realize that the lowest price isn't always the best deal if it means sacrificing quality.

"They will try to get the lowest price they can for the service they want," Ray says. "When they find they can no longer get the services they need, we see them willing to pay more." The level of service required usually depends on the type of facility.

"The people who really care a lot about their buildings are people who have important and demanding clientele in them, or a company that has a top executive who operates from that building who says cleaning is important to him," Ray says. Branch offices may be more focused on price than service, although they're usually willing to pay extra to have the place polished before a visit from a headquarters big shot.

Beware!

Until you've developed some skill at estimating charges, be careful about committing yourself to long-term contracts. If you accidentally bid too low, you don't want to have to do the job for a year or more at a loss.

Although much of the bidding process seems to be centered on pricing, be sure to emphasize the quality of your service and the value you provide. However, you must deliver what you promise, so never promise more than you can deliver.

Recognize your abilities—and your limitations. When you bid on a job, be sure you can handle it. Ask about the customer's special needs, and pay attention to details. Courtesy, genuine interest in meeting the customer's needs, and fair pricing will set you apart from the competition and help you build a reputation as a responsible operator.

Visit your prospective customers' sites and don't give an estimate until after you've seen the condition of the facility and have discussed with the client which services you'll provide. Never just "guesstimate" over the phone; you could lose the opportunity to make a serious bid if your figure is too high, or the customer may question your integrity if your phone quote is

Tip...

Smart Tip

Even though you may not want to be in the disaster restoration business, your crew may be the first ones on the scene in the event of a broken water pipe or other problem. Be flexible, and do what you can to help your customers when they need you, even if it's beyond your normal service package.

significantly lower than the final bid you make after you find out what the job really entails.

Ray says his normal approach is to work with property managers to establish the customers' preferred procedures before putting together a proposal. Usually they'll have put together a set of cleaning specifications, but you may need to ask how they want particular tasks handled, such as cleaning an office that has a lot of knickknacks, or what your responsibility is if people leave papers out on their desks at night (obviously, this happens often). You may want to establish a schedule for certain chores, such as rotating things that don't need to be done every night to balance the overall workload.

Estimating a Job

The first step in preparing an estimate is to identify the variables that will affect the time it takes to perform the required cleaning work (use the "Estimate Form" on page 57). Those variables may include:

- Size, in square feet, of the area to be cleaned
- Layout of the facility
- Number of employees
- Construction materials (carpeting, tile, glass, etc.)
- Location and position of furniture, equipment, appliances, etc.
- Number of offices, restrooms, and fixtures to clean
- Location of storage areas
- Areas requiring special attention

Main Floor

Let's get down to the nitty-gritty. Follow these instructions for floor cleaning, and your customers will sing your praises.

Stripping Old Wax and Dirt

1. Clear the floor of all obstacles, such as chairs, wastebaskets, and other movable items.
2. Sweep, dry-dust, or vacuum the floor completely.
3. Remove any heavy spot, dirt, or gum with a putty knife.
4. Mix the wax stripper and hot water according to the manufacturer's recommendations.
5. Apply the solution to the floor with a mop, and let it stand for a few minutes.
6. Scrub the floor with a scrub brush, steel wool pad, or nylon pad, depending on how much dirt and/or wax you have to remove.
7. Mop up the dirty solution.
8. Rinse the mop well and pick up any remaining solution with clean water.
9. Let the floor dry thoroughly.

Helpful Hints

○ Remove dirt in corners and along baseboards.
○ Wipe up any splashes on the walls, furniture, and baseboards.
○ Never allow water to stand on a tile floor; tile that stays wet too long may start to lift.
○ Don't attempt to scrub more than 100 square feet at once.

Waxing the Floor

1. Make sure the floor is clean.
2. Apply an even coat of wax or finish with a strong mop or wax applicator.
3. Wax evenly.
4. Let the wax dry for about 20 minutes. Apply a second coat if necessary.
5. Buff the floor if you use natural carnuba wax.

Helpful Hints

○ If you use a polymer finish, make sure to remove all old wax, resin finishes, and soap scum from the floor. Polymers won't adhere properly to natural waxes.

Main Floor, continued

❍ Don't apply wax with dirty applicators.

❍ Don't use an oily sweeping compound on floors.

❍ Don't let wax wear out in high-traffic spots. Touch up these spots from time to time.

❍ Don't let polish build up along baseboards.

- Availability and location of electrical outlets
- Frequency of duties
- Hours during which cleaning can take place

Floors are always a major consideration. They may require as much as 60 percent of your time. If floors are carpeted, how often will they need shampooing? If they aren't carpeted, how often will they require scrubbing and refinishing? A fully carpeted office building will take one-half to one-third of the time to maintain than a completely tiled one will. A tiled floor is more costly to maintain because it requires more labor and more chemicals to keep it clean and polished. Another time-consuming task is cleaning glass surfaces. The more you have to clean, the longer it will take.

You also need to consider how crowded the area is. The more crowded it is, the longer it will take to clean. Scrubbing and polishing an empty ballroom floor will take much less time than cleaning an average office with the same floor space. Along with how much furniture is in the rooms, take a look at the amount of clutter. The greater the clutter on desktops, filing cabinets, window ledges, coffee tables, counters, bookcases, etc., the more time it will take to dust, because you must move these items to clean both the item itself and the surface it's on.

Confirm whether cleaning windows and window shades will be included in your contract. If so, calculate the dimensions of the windows and consider the accessibility from both sides. Window cleaning can be time-consuming; you may want to avoid this task or subcontract it to a specialist.

Once you've surveyed the premises, the next step is to map out specific jobs, deciding

Smart Tip

Tip...

When putting together a bid, don't use the phrase "as needed" when describing task frequencies. Be specific about when various tasks are needed and what criteria are used to determine the need.

which tasks each worker or subcontractor will perform. Determine as best you can the time it will take to do the work, and don't forget the time needed to set up your equipment and supplies, and to put things away. If you plan to supervise or do part of the work yourself, be sure to include your time as part of the labor cost in your final estimate.

When you've figured out the number of hours required for your personnel to do their jobs according to the customer's specifications, you can calculate labor costs. If you're bidding on a job that calls for a monthly fee, figure the number of hours each worker will work in a month. If the job needs to be done five times a week, figure 21 workdays in a month. If it's to be done three times a week, figure 13 workdays in a month. Then multiply the wage rate for each worker by the number of hours you schedule for the job.

Next, calculate the cost of supplies. If you don't have actual cost records, estimate your supplies cost as a percentage of labor. Later, as you do more business and develop records, you can prepare estimates based on actual costs. This process is explained in detail in Chapter 9.

There are times when it will be to your advantage to offer premium or reduced pricing. When a customer wants immediate results and requests extended hours or more services, charging extra is reasonable and should be expected. (If the customer thinks you should provide these extra services for free, you need to consider whether this is a customer you really want to have.)

A long-term project with its accompanying long-term income or projects that may lead to lucrative follow-up business may warrant discounts. In such cases, you can consider a discount as an investment or even as part of your marketing costs.

Be sure you have a sound reason for any deviation from your normal pricing structure. If you arbitrarily decrease your rate, clients may believe you were overcharging them in the first place. When you give a discount, be sure your client understands that you have made a well-thought-out business decision and that you expect a return on your decision.

Be Prepared to Answer Questions

Purchasers of janitorial services are usually professional buyers who are accustomed to negotiating commercial product and service contracts. You'll impress them if you're prepared to provide the following information about your company:

- *How long you've been in business.* When you're new, emphasize the preparation and planning that has gone into developing your operation. If you have experience working for another cleaning company, stress that as well.

- *Training program.* Explain how you and your employees are trained to deliver top-notch service. If you have specific certification areas, such as in blood-borne pathogens, be sure to point that out.

- *Insurance.* Provide proof of liability insurance, workers' compensation coverage, and bonding.

- *Customer support.* Describe your support program, including whom the customer can contact with questions or problems, and what hours you're available.

- *Billing.* Explain your billing policies and procedures. Most commercial clients prefer paying monthly.

- *Equipment and materials.* Describe the modern equipment and quality cleaning products you provide that help your customers maintain their company image.

- *Supplies.* Discuss your program of providing disposable supplies such as paper towels, toilet tissue and seat covers, hand soap, plastic trash liners, etc. Be sure your pricing in this area is competitive.

- *Security.* Describe the measures you employ to assure your customers that you're responsible and can be trusted with keys and access to their premises after hours.

- *Attire and company identification.* Explain your uniform and employee identification program.

- *References.* Provide a client list and contact information so prospective customers can verify your service history and integrity.

Beware!
Workers' performance often deterio-rates after 6 to 12 months on the job. At this point, employees may either quit or need increased supervision.

Cash Flow Issue

Unlike many other types of cleaning businesses, janitorial services typically don't generate immediate cash flow. It will probably be at least 60 days or longer before you can write your first paycheck to yourself. You may get some one-time jobs like cleaning vacant homes, offices, or apartments for cash payment, but your most important source of income will be facilities you clean on a regular basis. You won't be paid for this work in cash. Some customers will pay on the 10th of the following month to earn a discount, while others will take the full 30 days to pay. You can expect to wait 45 to 50 days after signing your first big contract before receiving any money. This is why your startup capital needs to include enough funds to operate for at least the first quarter while you wait to start generating revenue.

If you start with insufficient cash on hand, you'll have a serious problem financing big accounts. You can't afford to bid on large jobs until you have the equivalent of at least two months' gross income from such a job in the bank so you can cover the labor costs for 60 days.

And unless you have an abundance of startup capital, you'll need to put every penny you possibly can back into your business to finance growth during your first critical year. You'll also work long hours, bidding during the day and supervising employees and even cleaning in the evening and on weekends.

Smart Tip

Your security system supplier will provide you with exterior signs and window decals to warn would-be intruders of the existence of an alarm. These notices are strong deterrents—better that a thief bypass your operation for the next than to suffer the break-in.

Security

Because most janitorial cleaning crews work at night, you have some security concerns that other types of cleaning businesses don't. You must take the necessary steps to provide a safe environment for your employees and to protect your equipment.

If you transport equipment in your vehicle, always park in a well-lighted area, and keep the automobile doors locked at all times, except when you're loading and unloading equipment and supplies. Consider installing an alarm on your vehicle; it will provide an additional level of security and may also earn you a discount on your insurance.

Do you keep your equipment in your home or garage? You may want to invest in a security system to prevent theft or vandalism. If you rent a mini-storage facility to store equipment and supplies, you probably won't be permitted to use a security alarm for your unit. However, most storage facilities have a gate with restricted access for their customers. Keep a sturdy lock on the door of your unit. Also, confirm with your insurance agent that the contents are covered.

Bright Idea

Provide training on various safety issues for your employees. For example, you may want to hold a session on how to remain aware of your surroundings to ensure safety at a cleaning site. Your local police department can help you with this training or refer you to a good source.

If you have a commercial office where you keep your equipment, investigate your area's crime history to determine the measures you need to take. Many commercial offices and storefronts have alarm systems already installed and included in the rental price. Most local police departments' crime prevention officers or community relations boards will provide you with information on the crime statistics in your area and prevention information.

Since your employees will often be arriving and/or leaving in the dark, be sure your parking facility is well-lighted, and establish a policy that employees must enter and leave the building in pairs.

Estimate Form

Date:
_____

Estimator:
_____

Referral source: Newspaper ad   Yellow Pages   Website   Other
_____

Customer name:
_____

Address:
_____

Phone: Emergency number:
_____

Service preferred: Daily   Weekly   Monthly   Other
_____

Days/hours preferred:
_____

Date services begin:
_____

Location of keys:
_____

Location of fuse boxes:
_____

Customer preferences:
_____

Carpets vacuumed:	Yes	No	Later (specify)
Windows cleaned:	Yes	No	Later (specify)
Walls washed:	Yes	No	Later (specify)
Floors stripped/waxed:	Yes	No	Later (specify)
Additional comments:	Tasks/room(s)/frequency		

Estimated time: Rate:
_____

Total:

Proposal Form

Proposal submitted to: _____ Date: _____

Address: _____

_____

_____

Job name and location: _____

_____

Job phone: _____

We hereby submit specifications and estimates subject to all terms and conditions as set forth below.

_____

_____

_____

_____

_____

_____

We hereby propose to furnish material and labor in accordance with above specifications for the sum of $ _____ (_____ dollars).

Note:
This proposal may be withdrawn by us if not accepted within _____ days.

Authorized signature: _____

Accepted: The above prices, specifications, and conditions are satisfactory and are hereby accepted. You are authorized to do the work as specified. Payment will be made as outlined above.

Signature: _____ Date: _____

Signature: _____ Date: _____

Carpet and Upholstery Cleaning Services

Sixty years ago, most homes had hardwood floors and commercial establishments had tile floors. Today, you're likely to find wall-to-wall carpeting in every room of the house, often even in bathrooms and kitchens. Businesses do everything with carpet but line the walls—and a few (some would say misguided) decorators have even done that

The on-location carpet cleaning industry was born because removing wall-to-wall carpet to clean it is highly impractical.

It's important to recognize that there has been a shift among consumers to alternative floor coverings. About 70 percent of floors in homes and workplaces are covered with carpets; the remainder are such materials as laminates, ceramic tile, stone, and hardwood. This means a clear opportunity for carpet cleaning services, especially those that are diversified and clean area rugs, upholstery, and those alternative floor coverings.

Most carpet cleaning services start as homebased businesses. As you grow, you may choose to move into a commercial location, but many highly profitable carpet cleaners never move out of their homes.

"This is a business that the average guy can really do without an enormous amount of education or expense," says Mike Blair, who owns AAA Prestige Carpet Care, a carpet and upholstery cleaning business in St. George, Utah. "It isn't for everybody. It's a physically and emotionally demanding business. You do it all when you're starting; you're the chief cook and bottle washer. But it's profitable enough."

Who Are Your Customers?

Every homeowner and business owner with installed carpeting and/or upholstered furniture is a prospective customer. Targeting a residential market will mean less in the way of startup costs and equipment since businesses typically require more than just having their carpets cleaned (you'll need more equipment to service them). However, because of the wide range of commercial businesses that use carpet and upholstery cleaning services, this is a lucrative market that is worth pursuing. Commercial operations that use carpet and upholstery cleaners include apartment buildings and condos, offices, schools, banks, restaurants, hotels, churches, bowling alleys, transportation terminals, and more.

Who Are Your Competitors?

Of course, you'll be competing against all the other carpet and upholstery cleaners in your area who target the same markets, but there are other sources of competition you need to be aware of.

Many commercial accounts prefer to contract with a janitorial service for their carpet cleaning and other miscellaneous cleaning jobs; it's easier for them to have a single source for these types of services. You need to convince these prospects that as a specialist, you'll do a better job. Or find out who their janitorial service is and work out a subcontracting deal with the service.

In the residential market, your primary competition (besides other carpet and upholstery cleaning services) will be the do-it-yourselfers. This includes people who rent carpet cleaning machines from local supermarkets, people who buy their own machines, and people who use spray-on-and-vacuum carpet cleaning products available in supermarkets and retail stores. One carpet cleaning service owner in Florida says that many of those spray-on products are the best sources of business he has, because they're often not used properly, don't generate the results people want, and may even leave carpets looking worse—which means he gets the call to do the job right.

Equipment

You have a wide range of choices when it comes to carpet cleaning and auxiliary equipment, and it could take you months to research them all. The following information should save you some time, but it's not a substitute for doing your homework and finding out what's on the market and how it works.

It's a good idea to avoid the older type of rotary-brush carpet cleaning machine. This is typically what's available for consumers to rent at retail stores. This type of machine is available in both consumer and commercial sizes, but even the large machines do an amateurish job—and therein lies the reason on-location carpet and upholstery cleaning businesses are booming. If homeowners and building superintendents were happy with poor results, they could hire any kid on the block to do their carpets and/or upholstery with a rented machine.

However, there's a demand for quality work—and if you provide it, you'll have a customer who will call you again and again. But you can't provide a better result than customers can achieve themselves if you don't use better equipment, and in most cases that means using commercial-grade machines.

Equipment manufacturers offer a wide range of styles and features with an equally wide range of prices and payment terms. Consider issues such as versatility—is the machine multi-functional (can it do more than just clean carpets?), and if so, what will you need in the way of accessories? What sort of warranty does the manufacturer provide? What about service contracts, training, and other support issues? Also, keep in mind that whether you choose truck-mounted or portable equipment, each of your service vehicles will need a carpet cleaning machine.

> **Tip...**
>
> **Smart Tip**
> Keep your back in mind when shopping for equipment. Look for tools and designs that reduce the stress on your back so you can work longer hours and be less tired at the end of the day.

Initial Equipment and Supply Checklist

- ❏ Carpet cleaners
- ❏ Carpet cleaning machine (truck-mounted unit)
- ❏ Carrying case for accessories
- ❏ Emulsifiers
- ❏ Groomers
- ❏ Horsehair brushes (for upholstery)
- ❏ Miscellaneous
- ❏ Pile brushes
- ❏ Pre-spray and fabric protector
- ❏ Signage
- ❏ Spotting brushes
- ❏ Utility brushes
- ❏ Wall cleaning machine

Before you can decide what type and brand of equipment is most appropriate for your business, you need to determine which cleaning methods you want to offer. Let's look at your options.

Cleaning Methods

Each system has its own merits, and the industry itself is divided over which is the "best"—wet shampooing, steam cleaning (which uses hot water extraction), or chemical dry cleaning, often followed by application of a fabric protector such as Teflon. Blair uses a combination of steam and chemical dry cleaning methods, depending on the circumstances and needs of the customer.

Upholstery can be dry-cleaned or shampooed, depending on the fiber content, using the same equipment you use for carpet cleaning, with some additional attachments, which, among other things, help guard against over-wetting. Or you can opt to purchase machines specifically designed for upholstery and drapery cleaning. As you do with carpet, follow upholstery cleaning by treating the furniture with a fabric protector to prevent future stains.

For carpets, use a pile brush to remove loose soil and precondition the carpet pile. Then use a high-powered vacuum for further soil removal, followed by one of these three methods:

> **Tip...**
>
> **Smart Tip**
> Take advantage of all the services your equipment vendors offer. Equipment manufacturers want their customers to be satisfied, and most will work with you as you learn their equipment. They usually provide training in the form of classes and seminars, both when you first purchase the equipment and later, as you hire new people. They'll also help if you encounter problems.

1. *Wet shampooing.* At one time, the rotary scrubber was the most popular cleaning apparatus. But if it did a good job, your business opportunities would be seriously reduced because, as we have already mentioned, rotary scrubbers are commonly available to rent at retail stores. These machines apply detergent solutions to the carpet by rotating brushes that ostensibly work on the top carpet fibers to prevent wetting the bottom of the carpet. A wet pickup extractor is then used to remove excess moisture and soil. Critics claim the agitation by the brushes loosens the surface soil but then drives it deep into the pile backing, and the soil later works its way back to the surface. Also, despite the extraction process, it can take a wet-shampooed carpet up to five days to dry, which is a major inconvenience to consumers. Other cleaning methods have made wet shampooing outdated.

2. *Steam cleaning.* The term "steam cleaning" is a misnomer because the process doesn't use steam. Steam applied to a carpet could damage some materials because of the high temperatures involved, or it might cause shrinkage.

   What's often called "steam cleaning" is actually a hot water extraction process, which involves the application of a detergent by a spray-on method, employing water heated to approximately 150 degrees. The hot solution is forced into the pile through controlled jet streams and immediately removed by a powerful vacuum. The process is also known as "deep soil extraction."

   This method of steam extraction is commonly used on residential pile carpets. The criticism that shrinkage is a factor only becomes a problem if a nonprofessional overwets the carpet. Even so, the quality of the results depends on the skill of the technician.

   Critics claim that when cleaning a carpet with heavy traffic patterns laden with dirt, such as those in offices, the steam process is insufficient, so shampooing is recommended. They also claim that steam extraction is more of a "wet" steam method; the carpet pile becomes saturated, and the washed-down soil works its way back to resoil the surface. After a steam cleaning, it typically takes from two to four hours (and sometimes up to six hours) for carpet to dry. Blair believes this method provides the best overall results of all the carpet cleaning methods.

3. *Chemical dry cleaning.* The name may give the impression that no moisture is used in this method, but that's not the case. The carpet is sprayed with a carbonated

Beware!
The average carpet cleaner will burn out in five years, says St. George, Utah, carpet and upholstery cleaning entrepreneur Mike Blair. The most common reason is failing to hire appropriate support staff as it becomes necessary. Another reason is not buying the right kind of equipment.

More than Carpet

Most carpet cleaning services do more than clean carpets. They also might offer:

- ○ Application of a fabric protector on carpet and upholstery
- ○ Carpet dyeing
- ○ Carpet restoration
- ○ Ceiling cleaning
- ○ Cleaning and restoration of other flooring materials, including tile, laminate, stone, and hardwood
- ○ Drapery cleaning
- ○ Flame-retardant treatment for drapes and upholstery
- ○ Odor control
- ○ Smoke damage cleanup and fire restoration
- ○ Spot and stain removal from upholstery
- ○ Upholstery cleaning
- ○ Wall cleaning
- ○ Water damage restoration

chemical that breaks down the soil, then buffed with a pad to pick up the dirt. Surface soil is removed, but if the vacuum is too weak, the sand and grit that grinds down the fibers remains, thus decreasing the life of the carpet. Critics of this method claim that while the carpet may appear cleaner, the dirt actually becomes smeared through the fibers, and most of it remains deep in the carpet. Many experts recommend that chemical dry cleaning be used only on an intermediate basis—in other words, between steam cleanings.

Chemicals

As wide as your selection for equipment is, your range of choices for solvents and cleaners is even greater. A good way to educate yourself in this area is to visit a local supplier where you can learn about the different types of chemicals available for cleaning carpets, draperies, upholstery, ceilings, walls, etc.

What you purchase depends on what you need to accomplish. There are spotters, liquid and powdered cleaners, sanitizers, stain-resistant coatings, concentrates, wrinkle removers (for drapery cleaning), deodorizers, anti-static protectors, and more.

With today's concern for the environment, many of these chemicals are supposedly nontoxic and/or biodegradable. The toxicity of chemicals and solvents can only be determined by visiting the supplier's warehouse and scrutinizing container labels. Many operators claim to use nontoxic chemicals, but the only way to be sure is to check with the Occupational Safety & Health Administration (OSHA). Most state laws require that every business or service possess a material safety data sheet (MSDS) that spells out the contents and level of toxicity (or nontoxicity) of each chemical agent used. Ask your supplier for copies of the MSDS for each product you're considering purchasing.

> ### Bright Idea
> Offer to clean the carpet at your place of worship at no charge for the opportunity to demonstrate the quality of your work. Be sure the arrangement includes displaying a flier or other information about your service in the building, and perhaps even an announcement in the newsletter.

Your chemicals and cleaning solutions will account for the majority of your inventory requirements, and you don't need to keep large quantities on hand. You can buy what you need to meet your customers' demands and avoid tying up your cash in excess inventory.

Larger carpet cleaning companies or those with multiple outlets or franchises typically keep a large inventory of cleaning supplies in storage at a central location. This allows them to take advantage of volume price breaks because their consumption rate justifies the investment in inventory and storage facilities. But this isn't the best strategy for a small startup operation.

In the beginning, buy your cleaning supplies in small amounts of about a gallon or so, and keep them in their original containers with the labels affixed. Depending on the type of equipment you have, you'll need different chemical compounds and solvents, such as special solvents for removing spots and stains. Your supplier can advise you on the types of solvents needed for removing specific kinds of stains.

Your initial supply, including the necessary brushes and applicators, should cost no more than a low of $500 to a high of $1,500.

Carpet Cleaning Basics

A great way to find out how to run your business in a way that will generate plenty of loyal, satisfied customers is to talk to people who have used carpet cleaning services.

Find out what they liked and didn't like, what made them happy and what caused dissatisfaction. Then use that information when formulating your operating procedures.

Some of the most common complaints:

- *Carpets taking too long to dry.* Customers don't mind waiting three or four hours for carpets to dry, but three or four days is too long.
- *Carpets not drying when promised.* Customers see this as a broken promise, and it makes them distrust you in the future. If you tell customers the carpets will be dry in a certain time, be sure they will.
- *Carpets still dirty after cleaning.* Inspect each job carefully to be sure you've gotten the carpets as clean as possible.

When the Damage Is Done

In addition to basic cleaning, many carpet cleaning services also do water damage restoration. Though the volume of this type of work is hard to predict, it can be lucrative and could help even out your workload during the year. And since you already have the ability to remove water from carpets, it's relatively easy to add this service to your business.

To offer water damage restoration, you must remove the water (which typically comes from a flood or a plumbing leak), dry the carpet with fans, and apply appropriate chemical compounds to sanitize and remove odors. St. George, Utah, carpet and upholstery cleaner Mike Blair recommends taking classes in the process before you begin marketing the service.

"Water damage restoration is a higher profit area that will sustain many carpet cleaners through the lean months of the winter and throughout the rest of the year," says Blair. "It's less competitive, meaning that it's a better-paid service, than a typical carpet cleaning business, which is very competitive."

Of course, there are reasons this service pays better than basic carpet cleaning. Water damage doesn't always happen during normal business hours, so you may be called out in the middle of the night to handle a job. The work can sometimes be dangerous; you'll risk exposure to molds, mildew, and potentially dangerous fungi. Also, combining water and electricity—which is necessary to get the work done—offers the potential for shocks.

Another profit center is in the rental of drying equipment, Blair says. Once you've done the primary water removal, you'll set up fans to blow the area dry, and you can charge for the use of that equipment.

- *Carpets not looking better after a professional cleaning.* Many do-it-yourselfers will hire a professional carpet cleaner expecting better results than they get from their own efforts. With your equipment and skill, you should be able to accomplish this.

- *Unprofessional service people.* Customers who are impressed with your sales presentation will be very distressed if your service technicians don't live up to your promises of professionalism and quality.

Stat Fact
In 2007 (the latest stats available), U.S. carpet manufacturers shipped 1.6 billion square yards of carpet (14.4 billion square feet), up from 97 million square yards in 1950, according to the Carpet and Rug Institute.

So what can you do to make sure your customers are satisfied and that they'll call you again and refer you to others?

- *Learn about carpet cleaning.* Cleaning a carpet isn't an exact science, and there's no one-size-fits-all formula that will work in every situation. Various materials require the use of different types of detergents, and different types of dirt and stains need different treatments. Your equipment manufacturer should provide you with guidelines that address just about every cleaning situation you'll encounter.

  Keep in mind that the companies that make carpet cleaning machines work closely with carpet manufacturers and will always be current on technological innovations, new carpeting materials, and improvements in the industry. They can keep you up-to-date on these matters. Most also offer training for you and your employees at either no charge or a nominal fee; your primary cost will be transportation to the training and lodging (if necessary), and it's well worth the investment.

- *Supervise your employees.* Don't just hire service technicians and turn them loose immediately to work on their own. Be sure they're trained and then accompany them on their jobs for at least the first few weeks (until you're certain they really know their jobs and can deal with both routine and unexpected situations). Then periodically drop in on a job in progress and follow up with your customers to be sure your service personnel are maintaining a high level of performance.

- *Estimate carefully.* This takes more time in the beginning, but it's critical that your estimates be accurate. When you overestimate, you'll lose jobs to your

Smart Tip
Take your vacuum and solution hoses to the furthest point in the house; then work backward toward the entry. Don't pull hoses around corners; doing so could damage wallpaper and woodwork.

competition; when you underestimate, you'll either lose money on the job or you'll irritate customers when you present a bill for more than you said it would cost. (See Chapter 9 for an explanation of how to set your prices.)

Smart Tip

Tip...

Use caution signs where needed and warn customers that smooth surfaces may be slippery after cleaning.

- *Avoid high-pressure sales tactics.* Try to close the sale on the first call, but don't use high-pressure techniques. If your prospect hesitates and says he wants to shop around, don't immediately lower your price. Instead, call back in a day or two and ask if a decision has been made. You shouldn't have to pressure your customers or cut prices if your rates are competitive; you've made an accurate estimate and you did a good job of selling your superior service on your first contact. Consumers tend to be impressed by an honest salesperson who's easy to decline, rather than having someone shove the sale down their throat. In the end, even if you don't get a sale, you'll have a better reputation—and you may get the call the next time.

Carpet Cleaning Specifics

Specific aspects of your operation will be determined by which type of cleaning you decide to do, which chemicals suit that particular cleaning method, whether you want to charge for moving furniture, if you give estimates over the phone or in person, etc. However, you can still follow a basic planned procedure in conducting your operation, from the customer's initial call to collecting your final payment.

Handling the Initial Service Request

When a new customer calls for an estimate, their first question is likely to be about price. They'll also want plenty of other information, such as whether you'll move furniture, how long it will take for the carpet to dry, and if you can handle special situations, such as pet stains and odors. Give honest, complete answers and stress why your cleaning methods are superior. If the customer fails to ask questions most people ask, volunteer the information anyway.

Visiting the Customer's Home

If you can't avoid giving an estimate over the phone and the customer commits to the sale during the call, set an appointment for the work to be done. If you're going

Good News Travels Fast

Once you're up and running, the major portion of your business will come from referrals and repeat customers, so pleasing your clients with quality work and top-notch service is critical. St. George, Utah, carpet and upholstery cleaner Mike Blair says 85 percent of his business comes from existing customers and referrals. "We have worked hard to establish a reputation for reliability in the community with property managers, realtors, homeowners, commercial establishments, and insurance professionals so that they call us and refer us," he says.

Because so much of your carpet cleaning business will come from referrals, be sure you market to people who can refer customers to you. Blair says one of the most effective marketing techniques he has used is to work with retail carpet salespeople. He gives them a demonstration of his cleaning skill, either in their showrooms or in their homes. "When they see the quality of our work, they are comfortable referring us to their clientele," he says. "Most of the carpet suppliers in town refer cleaning to us, and we work hard to keep that relationship alive." He also maintains relationships with residential and commercial property management companies, which can both use his services in the properties they manage, as well as refer other customers to him.

out to do the estimate in person, set an appointment that's convenient for the customer with the understanding that if the estimate is acceptable, you'll be prepared to do the work at that time.

When you arrive at the home, calculate the square footage of the areas to be cleaned. Check for especially soiled areas that may need extra pre-spotting and/or conditioning. If you think certain areas will need extra work and, as a result, will cost more to clean, be honest about it upfront. Your customer will greatly appreciate knowing this before, rather than after, the bill is written up.

Writing the Invoice

On the invoice (or service order), list the specific tasks you'll perform, as well as each room and its dimensions. If you have to pre-spot and specially treat any areas, note this.

Smart Tip
Tip...

Remind customers that you have to leave the door slightly open so they'll be sure to supervise small children or confine their pets.

▲

Next to each task, list the price; then total the charges. Have the customer sign and date the invoice before you start to work.

Your invoice should also include the estimate date, job date, day of the week, what time the job is to be performed, a job number, and the customer's address and telephone numbers (home, work, and cell). Make this task easy on yourself: Use the "Service Order/Invoice Worksheet" on the next page.

Performing the Service

With the paperwork done, you're ready to begin the job. First, move whatever furniture you need to and have agreed to. Do any pre-treating and conditioning. Then shampoo the carpet following the equipment manufacturer's instructions.

After cleaning, carefully put the furniture back. Use foam blocks or some other shield to protect wood pieces from damp carpet. Tell the customer how long it will take for the carpet to dry; suggest that they keep fans and/or air conditioning units on to help speed the process. You may want to invest in a dryer as an additional service to your customers. Collect payment under the terms you agreed on when you made the estimate (cash, check, or credit card). Note the payment on the invoice and give the customer a copy. You may want to give the customer some advice on caring for their carpet, and tell them you'll be in touch in about six months to schedule their next cleaning.

> **Smart Tip** *Tip...*
>
> Place a furniture pad under your hoses when they're stretched across wood and tile floors to prevent scratches from the couplers.

Furniture Cleaning Specifics

A significant percentage of people who are having their carpets cleaned want their upholstered furniture cleaned at the same time. Most carpet cleaning systems include tools for cleaning upholstery, but it's important that you understand the intricacies involved before you provide this additional service.

Inspecting Furniture Before Giving an Estimate

You need to determine the overall condition of the furniture and the best cleaning method to use. Ask if the piece has ever been professionally cleaned and, if so, when and how. Also ask if the customer has ever done any spot cleaning, and have them show you the areas involved. Find out how old the piece is, what the material is made of, and if it has ever been reupholstered.

Service Order/Invoice Worksheet

Customer name: _____

Primary contact: _____

Address: _____

City: _____ State: _____ Zip: _____

Home phone: _____ Work phone: _____

Cell phone: _____ Email: _____

Date of estimate: _____

Date of work performed: _____

                                    Date   Day   Time

Job number: _____

Areas to be cleaned:

Rooms: _____

Dimensions: _____

Square feet: _____

Total rooms: _____ Total square feet: _____

Work to be done: _____

_____

_____

_____

_____

_____

_____

_____

Total: _____

Customer signature: _____ Date: _____

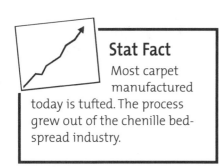

Stat Fact
Most carpet manufactured today is tufted. The process grew out of the chenille bedspread industry.

As you inspect the furniture, look for a recommended cleaning label; if it has one, follow those instructions. Note the overall condition of the fabric, check the back and arms for body oils and soil, check skirts and corners for shoe polish and scuff marks, check sides and back for dust or dirt filtration from exposure to air vents, examine heavily used areas for fabric fraying or thinness due to wear, look at both sides of cushions for stains or spots that may require special attention, unzip cushion covers and check the foam material inside for ink or marker that may have bled through. In homes with pets, look for pet oils, hair, and other stains. Confirm the sturdiness of all legs before moving the piece. Pretest to determine color-fastness and shrinkage risk.

Writing Your Estimate

Make notes on your invoice or work order of all problem areas, such as loose buttons, tears, holes, burns, shaky legs, and stains, and bring these imperfections to the customer's attention. Calculate your estimate, based on the cost of labor, supplies, overhead, and desired profit, and present it to the customer. See Chapter 9 for general price ranges of items you're likely to be cleaning. Before you begin, have the customer sign the work order, acknowledging that they're aware of the condition of the furniture.

Cleaning Furniture

Generally speaking, you should follow the furniture manufacturer's cleaning instructions, which are usually listed on a tag attached to the item. If there's no tag, use the procedures recommended by the equipment and chemical manufacturers.

Position the furniture toward the center of the room, away from walls and other furniture, and on pads to prevent overspray on floors, carpets, and other pieces. Most upholstered furniture can be wet-cleaned. In that case, begin by vacuuming to remove loose dirt and debris. Pre-spray and brush with a nylon brush to loosen embedded dirt; then clean. After cleaning, use a thick towel to wipe down furniture to remove

Smart Tip _Tip..._
The weight of heavy pieces of furniture can cause indentations in carpet. Encourage your customers to use furniture glides or cups under the legs of heavy pieces, or to periodically move furniture a few inches backward or sideways so the weight isn't concentrated in one place. To remove depressions, the Carpet and Rug Institute advises working the carpet pile back into place with your fingertips or the edge of a spoon, then dampening the area and heating it with a hair dryer, working the fibers with your fingers or a spoon.

residues and quicken the drying time. Wipe off any exposed wood. Arrange cushions on brown paper for drying, and be sure they're not touching each other.

If you're dry-cleaning furniture and drapes, be sure the area where you're cleaning is well-ventilated. Use the same procedure for positioning and preparing furniture; then follow the chemical manufacturer's cleaning recommendations.

Cleaning Drapes

As you do with furniture, reinspect drapes for spots or damage and bring those details to your customer's attention before you begin cleaning. Dust the surrounding areas; then vacuum drapes thoroughly, paying special attention to pleats or other areas where dust or dirt may have collected. Use a drapery board to prevent overspray on walls and windows. Take care to remove all solvent when finished; then towel the pleats to remove any remaining soil and help set and realign the pleats. Lined drapes may be cleaned on both sides; if you do this, adjust your price accordingly.

Other Cleaning Businesses

W e've discussed the most common cleaning services, but there are many more niche cleaning businesses you may want to consider, either as stand-alone operations or as companion businesses to your primary cleaning company. This chapter is designed more as an introduction to these specialty services rather than a comprehensive guide to actually providing them. They all require varying levels of training, skill, and equipment, and you'll need to do additional research on the areas that interest you. On top of the information here, there are resources in the Appendix that can help you with more data.

Smart Tip

Tip...

To tell which side of the window a streak is on, pull the squeegee down when you're cleaning the outside of the window and across when you're working on the inside. The direction of the streak will tell you which side it's on.

Window Cleaning

While some residential cleaning and janitorial services clean windows as part of their service, windows are a cleaning industry specialty. If you like working outside and you don't mind heights, window cleaning could be the perfect opportunity.

Some window cleaners charge by the pane (a piece of glass framed on all sides by wood or metal)—typically $4 to $8 each. Others charge by the job, using an hourly labor rate of $25 to $35 (and in some areas, up to $70 per hour) to calculate their fees.

Let It Shine

The basic equipment and supplies you need to get started in the window cleaning business include:

- Bucket with handle
- Cleaning agents
- Extension ladder
- Extension pole
- Scrapers and spare blades
- Soft, lint-free cloths (chamois)
- Sponges
- Squeegees
- Tool belt or holster
- Towels

If you're doing window cleaning as part of new construction cleanup, you'll need a vacuum cleaner to clean dirt and debris from the window tracks.

Window cleaning is more than just removing dirt. Windows often have tape or glue on them, or they've been painted over completely to block out light. In the case of the latter, test-clean a small part of the window to see how difficult the job will be before you quote a price.

It's a good idea to start your window cleaning service by targeting one- and two-story office buildings, storefronts, and homes. As you become established and your skill level increases, you can expand to taller buildings. High-rise window cleaning requires an extra level of skill to ensure the health and safety of above-ground workers. You'll need a controlled descent system for access to exterior high-rise windows. There are a variety of excellent systems on the market; never purchase and use any system without thorough training by the manufacturer.

Disaster Cleaning and Restoration

Many carpet cleaning and janitorial service companies do disaster cleaning and restoration for their customers, but this is a specialty area in its own right. You'll need special knowledge in fire, water, and smoke damage cleaning and restoration that's beyond the scope of this book.

Once you're trained, you can work with insurance adjusters and other contractors to provide all or part of the services needed. The Restoration Industry Association (see Appendix for contact information) offers training programs to help you develop the expertise necessary to provide this service.

Blind Cleaning

Mini-blinds aren't as trendy as they once were, but they are still common fixtures in homes and offices. Venetian blinds have enjoyed a resurgence in popularity, and many consumers are choosing interior shutters as window treatments. Along with vertical blinds and pleated shades, all these window coverings attract dust and need frequent cleaning—and the occasional pass with a feather duster isn't enough to keep them looking their best.

Without the proper equipment, cleaning blinds can be time-consuming and labor-intensive. Special blind-cleaning equipment (see this book's Appendix for equipment sources) can

Tip...

Smart Tip

After cleaning a window, seal it with protectants to prevent repeat staining and to make the next cleaning easier.

77

▲

Safety First

No matter what type of cleaning you're doing, always take proper safety precautions. For example, protect eyes from accidental splashes of harmful chemicals by wearing glasses or goggles. When working with acids, wear acid-resistant gloves. When working on construction sites or cleaning building exteriors, hard hats may be appropriate. The Occupational Safety & Health Administration (OSHA) can help you take the proper steps to create a safe working environment for yourself and your employees.

speed up the labor process and allow you to offer this service at an affordable price. You'll need to learn how to quickly and efficiently take down and rehang blinds, as well as operate your equipment.

As window coverings, blinds outnumber drapes 5-to-1, which means the need for blind cleaning is strong and likely to continue to grow.

Pressure Washing

Pressure washing can be added to an existing cleaning business or operated as an independent company for a modest initial investment. Some of the more common uses of pressure washing equipment include cleaning and maintenance of residential and commercial buildings, walkways, parking lots, heavy equipment and vehicles, truck and automobile fleets, trailers, engines, warehouse floors, machinery, kitchen areas, and sanitary areas.

Restroom Cleaning

Particularly in large public buildings, sports stadiums and arenas, and schools, there's a tremendous need for restroom cleaning, and companies that specialize in this work are busy and profitable. Businesses want to provide clean, pleasant, fresh-smelling restrooms for their employees and customers, and they're willing to hire specialists to get the results they need.

You'll clean and sanitize restrooms on a regular schedule and stock the facilities with soap and paper supplies as requested by your customers. You may work directly for the property owner or manager, or you may subcontract through a janitorial service.

Chimney Sweeping

Few things are more appealing to the senses than a crackling fire on a cold winter night. Even with central heat, many people still use their fireplaces. This means the chimneys need to be cleaned. The demand for chimney sweeping goes beyond residential fireplaces. The chimney sweep—or chimney service professional—aids in the prevention of fires, carbon monoxide intrusion, and other chimney-related hazards that can be caused by fireplaces; wood stoves; gas, oil, and coal heating systems; and the chimneys that serve them.

The basic task of a chimney sweep is to clean chimneys. That process includes removing the hazard of accumulated and highly combustible creosote produced by burning wood and wood products, eliminating the buildup of soot in coal- and oil-fired systems, and getting rid of bird and animal nests, leaves, and other debris that may create a hazard by blocking the flow of emissions from a home-heating appliance. Though the highest demand for chimney sweeps is in cold-climate regions, this is a service that's needed throughout the country. You should enjoy working outside and be comfortable with heights, because you'll spend a lot of time on roofs.

> **Smart Tip** _Tip..._
> When preparing your window-washing solution, add a few drops of cleaning solution to your bucket after you've filled it with water. Adding too much solution, or adding it before you fill the bucket, will create piles of suds, which inhibit quality work.

> **! Beware!**
> New ladders include instructions for safe use. No matter how tempting it may be to take a shortcut, always follow the manufacturer's directions.

In addition to cleaning, chimney sweep services may also offer repairs and parts such as chimney caps that protect the chimney from water, leaves, debris, and animal intrusion. A chimney sweep's customer base is both residential and commercial. Training and certification are available through the Chimney Safety Institute of America (see the Appendix for contact information).

Ceiling and Wall Cleaning

Ceilings and walls trap odors, smoke, oils, cooking grease, films, nicotine, dust mites, and many more unsanitary pollutants. These contaminants can reduce light by

The Stain Game

Because window stains can have a variety of causes, they require different cleaning approaches. Here are some common problems window cleaners encounter; to tackle them, talk to your window cleaning chemical supplier and ask for the most appropriate product.

○ *Everyday grime.* Windows are subject to exterior climatic conditions such as pollution, acid rain, and automobile exhaust. Inside, they can be abused by smoking, office equipment emissions, heating and air conditioning fumes, and fingerprints. To clean these films from transparent glass surfaces, you need a cleaning solution designed to reduce squeegee drag that will not bleed, dry, or streak and is strong enough to remove the dirt and grime.

○ *Oxidation.* When metal is exposed to rain and humidity, it gradually deteriorates and causes a process called oxidation. When this occurs near a window, it can penetrate or cling to the glass and is often called etching, hazing, or screen burn. You'll see it most often on windows that are covered by metal screens or surrounded by metal frames.

○ *Hard water stains.* When rainwater travels over concrete or precast surfaces, it can carry tiny particles from that surface onto the window. The dried rainwater leaves behind mineral deposits that are difficult to remove. Similar stains result from acid rain and irrigation systems.

○ *Overspray.* This occurs in new buildings or when various types of exterior maintenance are done. Typically, windows are stained with paint, glue, tape, caulking, and waterproofing overspray. Cleaning overspray often requires a combination of chemicals and razor scraping.

as much as 60 percent, dull the appearance of a facility, and contribute to an unhealthy environment. Cleaning ceilings and walls is far more cost-effective than painting or replacing them. In fact, replacing a ceiling can cost up to 100 times more than cleaning it, and the replacement process is slow, messy, and extremely inconvenient. Besides being part of standard building maintenance, various ceiling and wall cleaning techniques may also be used in disaster restoration work.

To clean ceilings and walls, you must learn how to work with various porous, nonporous, and semiporous surfaces to remove pollutants without damaging the appearance or function of the surface. Most vendors of ceiling and wall cleaning equipment offer training courses in the proper use of their equipment and chemicals.

Post Death and Trauma Cleaning

Cleaning up after someone has died, whether the death was from natural causes, suicide, or homicide, requires an in-depth understanding of biohazards, a capacity to cope with being regularly confronted with trauma scenes, and a tremendous amount of compassion.

Post death and trauma cleaning services are usually called in after a homicide, suicide, unattended death, or a non-fatal trauma where property has been contaminated by blood or other bodily fluids and tissue. "It's gross. We deal with blood and body fluids, and maggots sometimes," says Benjamin Lichtenwalner, co-founder of Biotrauma Inc. in Gainesville, Georgia. Because of the potential health risks, it's critical that the job be done properly and thoroughly.

An estimated 32,000 suicides and 17,000 homicides occur in the United States each year, leaving behind traumatized survivors and contaminated homes and businesses. In most cases, your clients will be the family of the deceased and you'll be paid by an insurance company. You may also be called to clean up commercial facilities after an accident or crime that has contaminated a property.

To get started, you'll need to make a substantial investment in training, equipment, and supplies. OSHA requires that all workers performing this type of remediation receive the proper training and vaccinations, and be properly equipped with protective gear and cleanup tools. EPA regulations dictate the disposition of hazardous wastes, so you'll need the proper tools and procedures to be in compliance. In addition to cleaning, you may also want to offer repair or replacement of structural components, such as carpet, flooring, cabinets, doors, and walls.

Developing Your Plan

Some entrepreneurs would rather walk on hot coals than sit down and write a business plan. Other would-be business owners get so caught up in planning every detail that they never get their businesses off the ground. You need to find a happy medium between these extremes.

Begin your venture with a written business plan. Writing your plans down forces you to think them through and gives you a chance to examine them for consistency and thoroughness. Whether you've got years of cleaning service experience behind you or you're a novice in the industry, you need a plan for your business. This chapter will focus on a few issues particular to planning cleaning service businesses, but they are by no means all you need to consider when writing your plan.

If you're excited about your business, creating a business plan should be an exciting process. It will help you define and evaluate the overall feasibility of your concept, clarify your goals, and determine what you'll need for startup and long-term operations.

> **Bright Idea**
>
> Update your business plan every year. Choose an annual date when you sit down with your plan, compare how closely your actual operation and results mirrored your forecasts, and decide if your plans for the coming year need adjusting. You'll also need to make your financial forecasts for the coming year based on current and expected market conditions.

This is a living, breathing document that will provide you with a road map for your company. You'll use it as a guide, referring to it regularly as you work through the startup process and during the ongoing operation of your business. And if you're going to be seeking outside financing, either in the form of loans or investors, your business plan will be the tool that convinces funding sources of your venture's worth.

Putting together a business plan isn't a linear process, although the final product may look that way. As you work through it, you'll likely find yourself jumping from equipment requirements to cash flow forecasts to staffing, then back to cash flow, on to marketing, and back to equipment requirements. Take your time developing your plan; whether you want to start a part-time residential cleaning service or build a major janitorial service, you're making a serious commitment, and you shouldn't rush into it.

Business Plan Elements

Though the specific content of your business plan will be unique, there's a basic format that you should follow. This will ensure that you address all the issues you need to, as well as provide lenders and investors with a document organized in a familiar way. The basic elements are:

- *Front matter*. This includes your cover page, a table of contents, and a statement of purpose.

- *Business description.* Describe the specific cleaning service business you intend to start, and list the reasons you can make it successful. This section should also include your business philosophy, goals, industry analysis, operations, inventory, and startup timetable.
- *Marketing plan.* Include an overview of the market, a description of your potential customers, a discussion of the advantages and drawbacks of your location, an analysis of the competition, and how you plan to promote your specific business.
- *Company organization.* In this section, describe your management structure, your staffing needs and how you expect to meet them, the consultants and advisors who will be assisting you, your legal structure, and the licenses, permits, and other regulatory issues that will affect your operations.
- *Financial data.* This is where you show the source(s) of your startup capital and how you're going to use the money. Include information on real estate, fixtures, equipment, and insurance. You'll also include your financial statements: balance sheet, profit-and-loss statement, break-even analysis, personal financial statements, and personal federal income tax returns.
- *Financial projections.* Take your financial data and project it out to show what your business will do. Include projected income statements for three years, cash flow statements for three years, along with worst-case income and cash flow statements to show what you'll do if your plan doesn't work.
- *Summary.* Bring your plan together in this section. If you're trying to appeal to a funding source, use this section to reiterate the merits of your plan.
- *Appendices.* Use this for supporting documents, such as your facility design and layout, marketing studies, sample advertising, copies of leases, and licensing information.

To Market, To Market

Market research provides businesses with data that allows them to identify and reach particular market segments and to solve or avoid marketing problems. A thorough market survey forms the foundation of any successful business. It would be impossible to develop marketing strategies or an effective product line without market research.

The goal of market research is for you to identify your market, find out where it is, and develop a strategy to communicate with prospective customers in a way that will convince them to buy from you.

Market research will also give you information you need about your competitors. You need to find out what they're doing and how that meets—or doesn't meet—the needs of the market.

One of the most basic elements of effective marketing is differentiating yourself from the competition. One marketing consultant calls it "eliminating the competition." If you set yourself apart because no one else does exactly what you do, then you essentially have no competition. However, before you can differentiate yourself, you first need to understand who your prospective competitors are and why your prospective customers might patronize them.

> ## Smart Tip
>
> When you think your plan is complete, look at it with a fresh eye. Is it realistic? Does it take into account all the possible variables that could affect your operation? After you're satisfied, ask two or three professional associates you trust to evaluate your plan. Use their input to correct any problems before you invest time and money.

In the case of janitorial and carpet cleaning services, you'll be able to find many of your competitors listed in the Yellow Pages of your local print or online telephone directory. For residential cleaning services, identifying your competitors are will likely be more challenging because many small independent operators may not have business listings.

However, an increasing number of residential cleaning services of all sizes are creating websites, which you can visit to find out the type of services they offer. Or you can simply call them, posing as a prospective customer, and ask about what they do, how they operate, and how much they charge.

To find out how to differentiate yourself, consider doing a survey of your competitors' customers. If you're starting a cleaning service that has primarily businesses for customers, this won't be a difficult proposition. Identifying customers is pretty easy in this arena. Most office buildings use janitorial services of some sort; call them and ask for the building manager. For businesses, look them up in the phone book and ask if they use a janitorial service. If they say yes, go ahead with the survey.

However, if you own a residential cleaning service, surveying your competition's customers is likely to be quite a bit trickier. You could survey apartment building managers, of course. And you can ask people you know if they use a service.

After you've compiled a list of prospective survey respondents, call them and explain that you're not selling anything but rather are doing a marketing survey of consumers of the particular type of cleaning service you plan to offer. If the customer is a business, ask if the work is handled in-house or contracted with an outside company.

Ask what they like about the service they're using and what they wish that service did differently or better. You may even ask what it would take to persuade them to change companies. Take detailed notes, and use that information to formulate your service package and policies. Knowing what consumers want will help you create a business that's unique in your market. Once you've started your operation, you can sell to the people and companies you surveyed.

Are You on a Mission?

At any given moment, most cleaning service business owners have a clear understanding of the mission of their companies. They know what they are doing, how and where it's being done, and who their customers are. Problems can arise, however, when that mission isn't clearly articulated into a statement, written down, and communicated to others. A mission statement defines what an organization is and why it exists. Writing it down and communicating it to others creates a sense of commonality and a more coherent approach to what you're trying to do.

Even in a very small company, a written mission statement helps everyone involved see the big picture and keeps them focused on the true goals of the business. At a minimum your mission statement should define who your primary customers are, identify the products and services you offer, and describe the geographical location in which you operate. For example, a residential cleaning service's mission statement might read something like this: "To provide customers in single-family homes in the Cobb County area with high-quality, personalized residential cleaning done by a well-trained, trustworthy staff." A janitorial service's mission statement might read: "To serve commercial accounts in the Chicago area by delivering high-quality, professional cleaning services that keep our clients' facilities clean and attractive."

A mission statement should be short—usually just one sentence and certainly no more than two. A good idea is to cap it at 100 words. Anything longer than that isn't a mission statement and will probably confuse your employees. To help you get started on your statement, use the "Mission Statement Worksheet" on page 88.

Once you've articulated your message, communicate it as often as possible to everyone in the company, along with customers and suppliers. Post it on the wall, hold meetings to talk about it, and include a reminder of the statement in employee correspondence.

It's more important to adequately communicate the mission statement to employees than to

> **Bright Idea**
> Your business plan should include worst-case scenarios, both for your own benefit and for your funding sources. You'll benefit from thinking ahead about what you'll do if things don't go as you want them to. You'll also increase the comfort level of your lenders and investors by demonstrating your ability to deal with adverse and potentially negative situations.

Mission Statement Worksheet

To develop an effective mission statement, answer these questions:

1. What products and/or services do we produce?_____

   _____

   _____

   _____

2. What geographical location do we operate in? _____

   _____

   _____

   _____

3. Why does my company exist? Whom do we serve? What is our purpose?____

   _____

   _____

   _____

4. What are our strengths, weaknesses, opportunities, and threats? _____

   _____

   _____

   _____

   _____

5. Considering the above, along with our expertise and resources, what business should we be in?_____

   _____

   _____

   _____

6. What is important to us? What do we stand for? _____

   _____

   _____

   _____

   _____

customers. It's not uncommon for an organization to try to use a mission statement primarily for promotion and secondarily to help employees identify what business they're in, but that doesn't work very well. The most effective mission statements are developed strictly for internal communication and discussion. Your mission statement doesn't have to be clever or catchy—just accurate.

Though your mission statement may never win an advertising or creativity award, it can still be an effective customer relations tool. One idea is to print your mission statement on a page, have every employee sign it, and provide every prospective and new customer with a copy. You can even include it on your brochures and invoices.

Finally, make sure your suppliers know what your mission statement is; it will help them serve you better if they understand what you're all about.

Smart Tip

Know someone who might be interested in investing in your business? Don't ask them for money right away. Ask them to read your business plan and give you some input. At best, they'll like the plan and offer to invest before you ask; at worst, you'll get some valuable input and they'll let you know they don't want to invest before you have to risk rejection.

Structuring Your Business

There's a lot to do when you start a business. This chapter will address some of the general issues you need to work out as you create an operating infrastructure for your company.

You may be tempted to rush through some of these steps. Don't. Take your time and give yourself a chance to consider all the possible consequences of each decision you make. As anxious as you probably are to get out there and work, taking the time to put together a solid foundation in the beginning will make it easier for you to build and grow in the long run.

Naming Your Company

One of the most important marketing tools you'll ever have is your company's name. A well-chosen name can work hard for you; an ineffective name means you have to work harder at marketing your company.

Your company name should clearly identify what you do in a way that will appeal to your target market. It should be short, catchy, and memorable. It should also be easy to pronounce and spell—people who can't say your company name may use you, but they won't refer anyone else to you.

When Mike Blair formed his carpet and upholstery cleaning company in St. George, Utah, the entire family got involved in the process. "We brainstormed every possible name we could think of—from the kinky ones to the slinky ones," he recalls. "Finally, what came out of it all was the word 'prestige.' It said what we wanted to do. We wanted a quality company; we didn't want to do a cheapo clean; we wanted to be a first-class company offering what our customers wanted to have." The result was AAA Prestige Carpet Care.

Though naming your company is without a doubt a creative process, it helps to take a systematic approach. Once you've decided on a name, or perhaps two or three possibilities, take the following steps:

- *Check the name for effectiveness and functionality*. Does it quickly and easily convey what you do? Is it easy to say and spell? Is it memorable in a positive way? Ask several of your friends and associates to serve as a focus group to help you evaluate the name's impact.
- *Search for potential conflicts in your local market*. Find out if any other local or regional business serving your market area has a name so similar that yours might confuse the public.

Bright Idea

Once you've narrowed your name search to three or four choices, test market your ideas by asking a small group of people who fit the profile of your potential customers what they think of the names you're considering. Find out what kind of company the name makes them think of and if they'd feel comfortable hiring a cleaning service with that name. Finally, get them to explain the reasoning behind their answers.

- *Check for legal availability.* Exactly how you do this depends on the legal structure you choose. Typically, sole proprietorships and partnerships operating under a name other than that of the owner(s) are required by the county, city, or state to register their fictitious name. Even if it's not required, it's a good idea, because that means no one else can use that name. Registration procedures vary among the states, so check with your county office. Corporations usually operate under their corporate name. In either case, you need to check with the appropriate regulatory agency to be sure the name you chose is available.

- *Check for use on the internet.* If someone else is already using your name as an address on the internet, consider coming up with something else. Even if you don't plan to put up a website or plan to use a variation of your name for your site, the use of your name by another company could be confusing to your customers.

- *Check to see if the name conflicts with any name listed on your state's trademark register.* Your state Department of Commerce can either help you or direct you to the correct agency. You should also check with the trademark register maintained by the U.S. Patent and Trademark Office (PTO), which is listed in this book's Appendix.

Once the name you've chosen passes these tests, you need to protect it by registering it with the appropriate state agency; again, your state Department of Commerce can help you. If you expect to be doing business on a national level—for example, if your long-term goal is to franchise your cleaning business—you should also register the name with the PTO.

Trademarks

Exactly what is a trademark? According to the PTO, "A trademark includes any word, name, symbol or device, or any combination, used, or intended to be used, in commerce to identify and distinguish the goods of one manufacturer or seller from goods manufactured or sold by others, and to indicate the source of the goods. In short, a trademark is a brand name."

Registering the name of your company as a trademark isn't essential, but it does offer some benefits. It gives notice to the public of your claim of ownership of the mark, a legal presumption of ownership nationwide, and the exclusive right to use the mark on or in connection with the goods or services set forth in the registration.

You can access information about applying for trademark protection and patents online or by contacting the PTO by phone. (See the Appendix for contact information.)

Protect Your Mark

Once you've established a trademark, you must use it or risk losing it. Trademarks not actively used for two or more years may be considered abandoned, which means someone else can use the mark and you'll have no recourse.

You also need to control your mark. Don't allow others to use your mark without your consent or without restricting what product or service it represents. Think about how companies like McDonald's and The Walt Disney Co. aggressively pursue unauthorized use of their trademarks. They understand how much they have to lose if they fail to control their marks.

If you discover someone using your mark without your authorization, consult with an attorney to determine the most appropriate and effective action.

Legal Structure

One of the first decisions you'll need to make about your new cleaning service business is the legal structure of your company. This is an important decision, and it can affect your financial liability, the amount of taxes you pay, and the degree of ultimate control you have over the company, as well as your ability to raise money, attract investors and ultimately sell the business. However, legal structure shouldn't be confused with operating structure. Your legal structure is the ownership structure—who actually owns the company. The operating structure defines who makes management decisions and runs the company.

A sole proprietorship is owned by the proprietor, a partnership is owned by the partners, and a corporation is owned by the shareholders. Another business structure, the limited liability company (LLC), combines the tax advantages of a sole proprietorship with the liability protection of a corporation. The rules on LLCs vary by state; check with your state's department of corporations for the latest requirements.

Sole proprietorships and partnerships can be operated however the owners choose. In a corporation, the shareholders typically elect directors who, in turn, elect officers who then employ other people to run and work in the company. It's possible for a corporation to have only one shareholder and to function as a sole proprietorship. In any case, how you plan to operate the company shouldn't be a major factor in your choice of legal structures.

So what goes into choosing a legal structure? The first question to ask is who is actually making the decision on the legal structure. If you're starting the company by yourself, you don't need to take anyone else's preferences into consideration. If there are multiple people involved, you need to consider how you're going to relate to each other in the business. You also need to consider the issue of asset protection and limiting your liability in the event things don't go as you expect.

Something else to think about is your target customers and what their perceptions will be of your structure. There's a tendency to believe that the legal form of a business has some relationship to the sophistication of the owners, with the sole proprietor as the least and the corporation as the most sophisticated. If your primary customer group is going to be other businesses, it might enhance your image if you incorporate. Homeowners may be comfortable hiring a residential cleaning service that's a sole proprietorship, but property managers and business owners are probably going to be more comfortable dealing with a corporation.

Your image notwithstanding, the biggest advantage of forming a corporation is in the area of asset protection and making sure that the assets you don't want to put into the business won't be liable for business debt. However, to take advantage of the protection a corporation offers, you must respect the corporation's identity. That means maintaining the corporation as a separate entity; keeping your corporate and personal funds separate, even if you are the sole shareholder; and following your state's rules regarding holding annual meetings and other record-keeping requirements.

Is any one of these structures better than another? Not necessarily. We found cleaning service business owners operating as sole proprietors, partnerships, and corporations, and they made their choices based on what was best for their particular situation. Choose the form that's most appropriate for your particular needs.

Do you need an attorney to set it up? Again, no. There are plenty of good do-it-yourself books and kits on the market, and most of the state agencies that oversee corporations have guidelines. Still, it's a good idea to have a lawyer look over your documents before you file them to make sure they're complete and will allow you to function as you want.

Finally, your choice of legal structure isn't an irrevocable decision, although if you're going to make a switch, it's easier to go from the simpler forms to the more sophisticated ones than the other way around. The typical pattern is to start as a sole proprietor and then move up to a corporation as the business grows. But if you need the asset protection of a corporation from the beginning, start out that way.

Licenses and Permits

Most cities and counties require business operators to obtain various licenses and permits to comply with local regulations. In general, the licensing requirements for most cleaning service businesses are minimal. Even so, while you're still in the planning stages, it's a good idea to check with your local planning and zoning department or city/county business license department to find out what licenses and permits you'll need and what's involved in obtaining them. You may need some or all of the following:

- *Occupational license or permit.* This is typically required by the city (or county if you're not within an incorporated city) for just about every business operating within its jurisdiction. License fees are essentially a tax, and the rates vary widely, based on the location and type of business. As part of the application process, the licensing bureau will check to make sure there are no zoning restrictions prohibiting you from operating.

- *Fire department permit.* If you use flammable materials or if your business is located in a commercial facility and is considered open to the public, you may be required to have a permit from the local fire department.

> ### Bright Idea
> Make photocopies of all your required licenses and permits, and keep them in a safe, fireproof place—ideally away from your office. Or scan them and store the digital files in a safe, off-site location. If anything happens to your records, you'll still have proof that you're operating legally.

- *Sign permit.* Many cities and suburbs have sign ordinances that restrict the size, location, and sometimes the lighting and type of sign you can use in front of your business. Landlords may also impose their own restrictions. Most residential areas forbid signs altogether. To avoid costly mistakes, check regulations and secure the written approval of your landlord before you invest in and post a sign.

Tax Driver

You may need to collect and remit sales tax on all or part of what you charge your customers. To find out what's required by your state, contact your state's Department of Revenue. This is also the department that usually issues resellers' permits, which may allow you to avoid paying sales tax on some of the materials you use to provide your services.

Laws on sales tax vary by state, and in many states, the amount of tax can vary by county and even city. Check with your state or your accountant to make sure you're operating in compliance with the law.

- *State licenses*. Many states require persons engaged in certain occupations to hold licenses or occupational permits. Often, these people must pass state examinations before they can conduct business. States commonly require licensing for auto mechanics, plumbers, electricians, building contractors, collection agents, insurance agents, real estate brokers, repossessors, and personal service providers such as doctors, nurses, barbers, cosmetologists, etc. It's highly unlikely that you'll need a state license to operate your cleaning service business, but it's a good idea to check with your state's occupation licensing entity to be sure.

Be sure to check with city, state, and county government offices to make sure you've got all the permits you need.

Professional Services

As a business owner, you may be the boss, but you can't be expected to know everything. You'll occasionally need to turn to professionals for information and assistance. It's a good idea to establish a relationship with these professionals before you get into a crisis situation.

Even though you may know something about the issue in question, you probably don't have all the expertise you need. After all, you're an expert at cleaning—not taxes or legal issues. It's a lesson Michael Ray, owner of Pro Building Services Inc. in Salt Lake City, learned the hard way. "I thought I could do my accounting myself for a time and still succeed," he says. "But I didn't have the skills for it, and taking accounting classes in college didn't qualify me to understand what I needed to know."

To shop for a professional service provider, ask friends and associates for recommendations. You might also check with your local chamber of commerce or trade association for referrals. Find someone who understands your industry and specific business and appears eager to work with you. Check them out with the Better Business Bureau and the appropriate state licensing agency before committing yourself.

As a cleaning business owner, the professional service providers you're likely to need include:

- *Attorney*. You need a lawyer who understands and practices in the area of business law, who's honest, and who appreciates your patronage. In most parts of the United States, there's an abundance of lawyers willing to compete fiercely for the privilege of serving you. Interview several, and choose one you feel comfortable with.

Be sure to clarify the fee schedule ahead of time, and get your agreement in writing. Keep in mind that good commercial lawyers don't come cheap; if you want good advice, you must be willing to pay for it. Your attorney should review all contracts, leases, letters of intent, and other legal documents before you sign them. They can also help you with collecting bad debts and establishing personnel policies and procedures. Of course, if you're unsure of the legal ramifications of any situation, call your attorney immediately.

Smart Tip

When dealing with your banker, always remember that the bank is profiting from your business and that you're entitled to be treated with the same courtesy and respect with which you treat your own customers.

- *Accountant.* Among your outside advisors, your accountant is likely to have the greatest impact on the success or failure of your business. If you're forming a corporation, your accountant should counsel you on tax issues during startup. On an ongoing basis, your accountant can help you organize the statistical data concerning your business; assist in charting future actions based on past performance; and advise you on your overall financial strategies regarding purchasing, capital investment, and other matters related to your business goals. A good accountant will also serve as a tax advisor, making sure that you're not only in compliance with all applicable regulations, but also that you don't overpay any taxes.

- *Insurance agent.* A good independent insurance agent can assist you with all aspects of your business insurance, from general liability to employee benefits, and probably even handle your personal lines as well. Look for an agent who works with a wide range of insurers and understands your particular business. This agent should be willing to explain the details of various types of coverage, consult with you to determine the most appropriate coverage, help you understand the degree of risk you're taking, work with you to develop risk-reduction programs, and assist in expediting claims.

- *Banker.* You need a business bank account and a relationship with a banker. Don't just choose the bank you've always done your personal banking with; it may not be the best bank for your business. Interview several bankers before making a decision on where to place your business. Once your account is opened, maintain a relationship with the banker. Periodically sit down and review your accounts and the services you use to make sure you're getting the package most appropriate for your situation. Ask for advice if you have financial questions or are having problems. If you ever need a loan or a bank reference to provide to creditors, the relationship you've established will work in your favor.

98

- *Consultants*. The consulting industry is booming—and for good reason. Consultants can provide valuable, objective input on all aspects of your business. Consider hiring a business consultant to evaluate your business plan or a marketing consultant to assist you in that area. When you're ready to hire employees, a human resources consultant may help you avoid some costly mistakes. Consulting fees vary widely depending on the individual's experience, location, and field of expertise. If you can't afford to hire a consultant, consider contacting the business school at a nearby college or university and hiring an MBA student to help you.

- *Computer expert*. If you don't know much about computers, find someone to help you select a system and the appropriate software—someone who will be available to help you maintain, troubleshoot, and expand your system as you need it. If you're going to pursue internet sales, use a professional web designer to set up and maintain your site. Just as you wouldn't do an unprofessional cleaning job, you shouldn't put up an unprofessional web page. Ask other business owners in your community for recommendations and always check references before hiring.

Create Your Own Advisory Board

Not even the president of the United States is expected to know everything. That's why he surrounds himself with advisors—experts in particular areas who provide knowledge and information to help him make decisions. Savvy small-business owners use a similar strategy.

You can assemble a team of volunteer advisors to periodically meet with you to offer advice and direction. Because this isn't an official or legal entity, you have a great deal of latitude in how you set it up. Advisory boards can be structured to help both with the direct operation of your company as well as keeping you informed on various business, legal, and financial trends that may affect you.

Use these tips to set up your board:

- *Structure a board that meets your needs*. Generally, you'll want a legal advisor, an accountant, a marketing expert, a human resources person, and perhaps a financial advisor. You may also want successful entrepreneurs from other industries who understand the basics of business and can view your operation with a fresh eye.

Smart Tip

Tip...

Choose professional advisors who want to take an active role in helping your business succeed. They should not only do what you ask but also take the initiative to offer suggestions about how you can increase sales and profits as well as operate more efficiently.

- *Ask the most successful people you can find, even if you don't know them well.* You'll be surprised at how willing people are to help another business succeed.

- *Be clear about what you're trying to do.* Let your prospective advisors know what your goals are and that you don't expect them to take on an active management role or to assume any liability for your company or for the advice they offer.

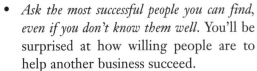

Bright Idea

Study business failures as well as successes. Understanding what caused other businesses—even those not related to the cleaning industry—to fail can help you avoid the same mistakes.

- *Don't worry about compensation.* Advisory board members are rarely compensated with more than lunch or dinner. Of course, if a member of your board provides a direct service—for example, if an attorney reviews a contract or an accountant prepares a financial statement—they should be paid at their normal rate because that's not part of their job as an advisory board member. However, even though you don't write them a check, keep in mind that your advisory board members will likely benefit from helping you in a variety of tangible and intangible ways. Being on your board will expose them to ideas and perspectives they may not otherwise have and will also expand their own networks.

- *Consider the group dynamics when holding meetings.* You may want to meet with all the members together or in small groups of one or two. It all depends on how they relate to each other and what you need to accomplish. Don't be afraid to vary your meeting structure or pattern as the circumstances require.

- *Ask for honesty, and don't be offended when you get it.* Your pride might be hurt when someone points out something you're doing wrong, but the awareness will be beneficial in the long run. Also, curb any impulse to be defensive and simply accept the input graciously.

- *Learn from failure as well as success.* Encourage board members to tell you about their mistakes so you can avoid repeating them.

- *Respect the contribution your board members make.* Let them know you appreciate how busy they are, and don't abuse or waste their time.

- *Make it fun.* You are, after all, asking these people to donate their time, so create a pleasant atmosphere.

- *Listen to every piece of advice.* Stop talking and listen. You don't have to follow every piece of advice, but you need to hear it.

- *Provide feedback to the board.* Good or bad, let the board know what you did and what the results were.

Insurance Issues

Insurance can be a tremendous challenge for cleaning service businesses. Many independent operators can't afford to purchase coverage, which puts them in a difficult Catch-22 situation if they're trying to get large accounts that require their suppliers to have certain levels of insurance. Of course, a very small company owned by one or two people who do all the work may not need insurance to cover employee theft and workers' compensation until they begin hiring employees. On the other hand, if you're doing something like high-rise exterior window cleaning, the building's owner will want to see proof that he's not going to be held liable if you're hurt on the job.

Having proper insurance is a good customer-relations move as well as a safety feature for your company. Having insurance shows your clients that you're a knowledgeable and serious business owner and that you're prepared to take responsibility for your employees' actions.

Issues of particular interest to cleaning services are liability coverage in case someone is injured as a result of your work or if something is damaged, and bonding to protect your customers if one of your employees steals something.

Your best strategy is to sit down with an insurance agent who understands the special needs of cleaning service businesses, discuss what's appropriate for your particular operation, and then make a final decision based on the benefits and costs of specific coverages.

> **Tip...**
>
> ## Smart Tip
> Sit down with your insurance agent every year and review your insurance needs; as your company grows, they are sure to change. Insurance companies are always developing new products to meet the needs of the growing small-business market, and it's possible one of these new policies is more appropriate for you.

Deliveries and Storage

When you're very new and small, it may be easier to run to your nearest supply house and pick up what you need in the way of chemicals and cleaning solutions. As you grow, it will be more efficient to have your suppliers deliver to you.

Whether the deliveries are being made by your supplier's truck or a commercial freight carrier, be sure to count and inspect every package before signing for the materials. Any shortages or external damage should be noted on the delivery receipt and claims filed promptly. If you find damage after the driver has left, notify the supplier and the carrier immediately.

▲

Store cleaning solutions and chemicals in a clean, dry space away from extreme temperatures. Follow the instructions on the product for any special storage requirements. Generally, metal shelves and metal cabinets are best for storing cleaning products.

Access to the storage area should be limited to supervisors and managers who are trained to use whatever inventory control methods you have in place. This is important both from a safety perspective and for the sake of accurate financial management.

Finally, as you use various products, be sure the empty containers are properly disposed of. As with use and storage, the manufacturers include instructions on the label if there are any special disposal requirements; be sure to follow their guidelines.

Cleaning service companies aren't likely to have much in the way of outgoing freight, but you'll probably use regular mail for functions such as marketing, invoicing, and other communications with customers and suppliers. For more information on mailing and shipping prices, check with the United States Postal Service.

The Hidden Profit-Eater

Freight is a variable expense that can be hard to predict but has a definite—and often significant—impact on your bottom line. As you shop for and build relationships with suppliers, consider where they're located and how much it will cost for you to receive their goods.

Track your freight costs carefully, and be sure each charge is accurate. It's a good idea to periodically check to make sure the weight of the shipment matches the weight you were charged for. And if your supplier prepays the freight charges and adds it to your invoice, verify that the rates have been correctly calculated.

If you buy primarily from local suppliers and pick up the merchandise yourself, you still need to consider the cost of getting the materials from their location to yours. In this situation, your time and vehicle expenses need to be considered as freight costs when calculating your cost of supplies.

Money Matters

In the small-business world, there are two key sides to the issue of money: How much do you need to start and operate, and how much can you expect to take in? Doing this analysis is often extremely difficult for small-business owners who would rather be in the trenches getting the work done than bound to a desk dealing with tiresome numbers. A dirty floor or dusty armoire may have more appeal than a budget that needs planning, but the budget is critical, because if your business isn't profitable, you won't be around to do any cleaning.

Sources of Startup Funds

Most of the cleaning service operators we spoke with used personal savings to start their businesses and then reinvested their early profits to fund growth. If you need to purchase equipment, you should be able to find financing, especially if you can show that you've put some of your own cash into the business. Beyond traditional financing, you have a range of options when it comes to raising money. Some suggestions:

- *Your own resources.* Do a thorough inventory of your assets. People generally have more assets than they immediately realize. This could include savings accounts, equity in real estate, retirement accounts, vehicles, recreation equipment, collections, and other investments. You may opt to sell assets for cash or use them as collateral for a loan. Take a look, too, at your personal line of credit. Many a successful business has been started with credit cards.

- *Friends and family.* The next logical step after gathering your own resources is to approach friends and relatives who believe in you and want to help you succeed. Be cautious with these arrangements; no matter how close you are, present yourself professionally, put everything in writing, and be sure the individuals you approach can afford to take the risk of investing in your business. Never ask a friend or family member to invest or lend you money they can't afford to lose.

- *Partners.* Using the "strength in numbers" principle, look around for someone who may want to team up with you in your venture. You may choose someone who has financial resources and wants to work side-by-side with you in the business. Or you may find someone who has money to invest but no interest in doing the actual work. Be sure to create a written partnership agreement that clearly defines your respective responsibilities and obligations.

- *Government programs:* Take advantage of the abundance of local, state, and federal

> **Bright Idea**
>
> Looking for startup cash? Consider a garage sale. You may have plenty of "stuff" you're not using and won't miss that can be sold for the cash you need to get your cleaning business off the ground. Another option for turning your things into cash is to sell them on sites such as eBay or Craigslist.

programs designed to support small businesses. Make your first stop the SBA, and then investigate other programs. Women, minorities, and veterans should check out niche financing possibilities designed to help these groups get into business. The business section of your local library is a good place to begin your research.

Setting Prices

Pricing can be tedious and time-consuming, especially if you don't have a knack for crunching numbers. Particularly in the beginning, don't rush through this process. If your quote is too low, you'll either rob yourself of some profit or be forced to lower the quality of your work to meet the price. If you estimate too high, you may lose the contract altogether, especially if you're in a competitive bidding situation. Remember, in many cleaning situations, you may be competing against the customer him- or herself; if your quote is high, he or she may think, "For that much money, I can do this myself."

Of course, you'll make mistakes in the beginning. For example, one residential cleaning service operator we spoke with started out quoting an hourly rate, but as she became more efficient and was able to clean faster, she realized it would be more profitable to charge by the job than by the hour. Charge for the value of your service, not the time you spend. It's also a good idea to charge what you would charge if you had employees, even at the very beginning when you're doing the work yourself. Some people make the mistake of undercharging when they start out just to get customers and then later on, when they grow and need to hire help, they aren't making enough money to pay that help. Also, if you are too cheap, customers will think you aren't experienced or don't do quality work. So don't underprice your services.

During the initial days of your operation, you should go back and look at the actual costs of every job when it's completed to see how close your estimate was to reality. Learning how to accurately estimate labor and properly calculate overhead will let you set a competitive pricing schedule and still make the profit you require.

To arrive at a strong pricing structure for your particular operation, consider these three factors:

1. Labor and materials (or supplies)
2. Overhead
3. Profit

> **Tip...**
>
> **Smart Tip**
> Don't set prices low just to get business when you're starting out. Customers who use you based solely on price will leave you for the same reason. Be sure your prices are competitive, fair, and high enough for you to make a reasonable profit.

Bill Me

You'll set your prices for specific upholstery cleaning jobs based on the condition of the items you're cleaning, the labor and materials required, and the profit you want to make. The ranges below will give you an idea what to charge.

Cushions only	$10–$15 each
Dining room chairs	$9–$20
Draperies	$2.50–$8.00 per pleat
Foot stools and ottomans	$10–$25
Love seats	$40–$140
Occasional chairs	$20–$30
Recliners	$35–$50
Sofas (depending on size)	$60–$196
Stools and benches	$12–$20
Toss pillows	$5–$10 each

If odor control is necessary, add 25 percent

Labor and Materials

Until you establish records to use as a guide, you'll have to estimate the costs of labor and materials. Labor costs include wages and benefits you pay your employees. If you're even partly involved in executing a job, the cost of your labor, proportionate to your input, must be included in the total labor charge. Labor cost is usually expressed as an hourly rate.

Overhead

Overhead consists of all the non-labor, indirect expenses required to operate your business. Your overhead rate is usually calculated as a percentage of your labor and materials. If you have past operating expenses to guide you, figuring an overhead rate isn't difficult. Total your expenses for one year, excluding labor and materials. Divide this number by your total cost of labor and materials to determine your overhead rate. When you're starting out, you won't have past expenses to guide you, so use figures that are accepted industry averages. You can raise or lower the numbers later to suit the realities of your operation.

Let's Make a Deal

You may have some prospective customers who honestly believe your quote is too high, others who make it a habit to never accept the first price as the final one, and still others who simply enjoy haggling. Whether you choose to negotiate is entirely up to you. Orlando residential cleaning service owner Fenna Owens starts and sticks with what she believes is a fair price. "If they don't like it, that's their prerogative," she says. "I don't usually go lower than what I think it should be."

If you charge less than what you think the job is worth or less than it will take for you to make a reasonable profit, the quality of your work and, eventually, the overall success of your company will suffer. It's difficult to turn down work, especially when you're first getting started, but sometimes it's better to decline an account than to take it on at a loss.

One effective negotiating technique is to reduce your price only when you take something out of the service package. When a prospective customer says her price is too high, Wanda Guzman in Orlando goes through what her quote covers and suggests removing some of the services to bring the price down. Or you can ask what the customers are willing to pay and tell them how much you'll do for that price.

Profit

Profit is, of course, the difference between what it costs you to provide a service and what you actually charge the customer. Figure your net profit into your estimate by applying a markup percent to the combined costs of labor, materials, and overhead. The markup percent will be larger than the actual percentage of gross revenue you'll end up with for your net profit. For example, if you plan to net 38 percent before taxes out of your gross revenue, you'll need to apply a markup of about 61.3 percent to your labor and materials plus overhead to achieve that target. (To determine your markup percentage, refer to the "Calculating Markup" chart on page 115.)

Setting Residential Cleaning Service Prices

Most residential cleaning services don't have particularly high overhead costs. Figure that overhead runs from 10 percent to 40 percent of your labor and materials, depending on the size of your operation, whether you're homebased or commercial-based, and the number of employees you maintain on your payroll.

Here's an example:

Overhead expenses	$5,220
Estimate of labor-and-materials cost	$51,240
Overhead rate ($5,220 ÷ $51,240)	10%

To calculate the cost of a single cleaning, the example looks like this:

Labor-and-materials cost	$45.00
Overhead (10% of $45)	$4.50
Subtotal of operating expenses	$49.50

Most residential cleaning service operators expect to net 10 to 30 percent of their gross revenue. To continue our example with a target of netting 20 percent before taxes:

Subtotal of operating expenses	$49.50
Net profit (25% of $49.50)	$12.38
Total price quoted to the customer	$61.88

Note that the $12.38 net profit ends up as 20 percent of $61.88 (which is the "selling price").

Setting Janitorial Service Prices

Overhead for a janitorial service is somewhat higher than for a residential service, typically ranging from 20 to 50 percent of labor costs.

Labor-and-materials cost	$353
Overhead (38% of $353)	$134
Subtotal of operating expenses	$487

Supplies typically run about 5 percent of labor, although Salt Lake City's Michael Ray

Smart Tip

When your customers want you to provide consumable supplies, bill them for the actual amount they use. Some customers may try to get you to include those items in your basic fee, but the consumption rate can vary so significantly that you may find it impossible to make a fair estimate.

says his goal is to keep them between 3 and 4 percent. Use industry averages to help you calculate your estimates until you have a history and can use actual expenses.

Here's an example of a bid on a job that will take two hours of labor per day, five days a week, at $8 per hour, and using an overhead rate of 38 percent:

Subtotal of operating expenses	$487
Net profit (28% of $487)	$136
Total price quoted to the customer	$623

Bright Idea

Providing consumable items such as bathroom tissue, paper towels, hand soap, feminine hygiene products, and trash can liners can be profitable for you and save your clients money. If you take the volume pricing you receive from your suppliers and mark it up slightly, you'll still make money, and your customers will likely get lower prices than they could negotiate on their own.

Most janitorial service operators expect to earn a net profit of 10 to 28 percent of gross sales. In our example, we want to yield a 22 percent net profit before taxes.

Note that the $136 net profit ends up as 22 percent of $623 (which is the "selling price").

Setting Carpet Cleaning Prices

Most carpet cleaning services charge by the square foot. Mike Blair says prices can range from 15 to 45 cents per square foot, depending on the particular market, the total services provided, and the ability of the cleaning company to communicate its value. It may take experimenting with pricing in your market to determine the optimum price level that your customers will perceive as fair and yet will still allow you to make an adequate profit.

In the carpet cleaning industry, overhead typically costs from 47 to 54 percent of your labor-and-materials cost.

Let's say you cleaned 2,144,800 square feet of carpet in one year. Our example looks like this:

Overhead expenses	$61,080
Estimate of labor-and-materials cost	$128,688
Overhead rate ($61,080 ÷ $128,688)	47.5%

Using an overhead rate of 47.5 percent as just computed, we can take our example to the next step and calculate the cost to clean one square foot of carpet:

Labor-and-materials cost	$0.06
Overhead (47.5% of $0.06)	$0.03
Subtotal of operating expenses	$0.09

The typical net profit for carpet cleaning businesses ranges from 30 to 45 percent of gross revenue. To calculate a net profit of 38 percent for our example, the numbers look like this:

Subtotal of operating expenses	$0.09
Net profit (66.7% of $0.09 or 40% of $0.15)	$0.06
Total price per square foot	$0.15
Price quoted to the customer for a 1,500-square-foot job ($0.15 x 1,500)	$225

If you compare the price of $0.15 above with the cost of labor and materials ($0.06) already estimated, you'll see that the quote is just a little more than double the labor charge. Some carpet cleaners use this ratio as a basis for determining price—they estimate their labor costs and then double that figure to arrive at their quotes.

Keeping Records

One of the key indicators of the overall health of your business is its financial status, and it's important that you monitor your financial progress closely. The only way you can do that is to keep good records. You may want to crunch your numbers manually. If not, there are a number of excellent computer accounting programs on the market. Ask your accountant for assistance getting your system set up. The key is to monitor your finances from the very beginning and keep your records current and accurate throughout the life of your company.

Keeping good records helps generate the financial statements that tell you exactly where you stand and what you need to do next. The key financial statements you need to understand and use regularly are:

- *Profit and loss statement* (also called the P&L or the income statement), which illustrates how much your company is making or losing over a designated period—monthly, quarterly, or annually—by subtracting expenses from revenue to arrive at a net result, which is either a profit or a loss

- *Balance sheet*, which is a table showing your assets, liabilities, and capital at a specific point. A balance sheet is typically generated monthly, quarterly, or annually when the books are closed.

Something's Afoot

The factor that has the biggest impact on the square foot rate for carpet cleaning is whether the property is empty or furnished. The next most important factor is the degree of soil and general condition of the carpet.

"How we distinguish the price has to do with the number of square feet and the number of furnishings we have to negotiate or don't have to negotiate," explains Mike Blair, owner of AAA Prestige Carpet Care in St. George, Utah. "If the property is empty, it's less in almost every application." The condition of the carpet, type of soil, and traffic patterns can also affect the time it takes—and therefore the cost—to clean.

You'll also want to consider the type of fiber in the carpet. "There are some unique fabrics that have to be considered," Blair says. For example, cleaning a valuable Oriental rug will cost more than the typical low-end carpet used in apartment complexes because of the expertise required.

- *Cash flow statement*, which summarizes the operating, investing, and financing activities of your business as they relate to the inflow and outflow of cash. As with the profit and loss statement, a cash flow statement is prepared to reflect a specific accounting period, such as monthly, quarterly, or annually.

Successful cleaning service operators review these reports regularly, at least monthly, so they always know where they stand and can quickly move to correct minor difficulties before they become major financial problems.

Billing

⚠ Beware!

Mail thieves operate even in the nicest of neighborhoods. If you receive checks in the mail, rent a post office box so you know they'll be secure.

If you're extending credit to your customers—and it's likely you will if you have corporate accounts or if you are in the janitorial business—you need to establish and follow sound billing procedures.

Coordinate your billing system with your customers' payable procedures. Candidly ask what you can do to ensure prompt payment; that may include confirming the correct billing address and finding out what documentation may be required to help the customer determine the validity of the invoice. Keep in mind that many large companies pay certain types of invoices on certain days of the month; find out if your customers do that, and schedule your invoices to arrive in time for the next payment cycle.

Most computer bookkeeping software programs include basic invoices. If you design your own invoices and statements, be sure they're clear and easy to understand. Detail each item and indicate the amount due in bold with the words "Please pay" in front of the total. A confusing invoice may be set aside for clarification, and your payment will be delayed.

Your invoice should also clearly indicate the terms under which you've extended credit. Terms include the date the invoice is due, any discount for early payment and additional charges for late payment. For example, terms of "net 30" means the entire amount is due in 30 days; terms of "2-10, net 30" means that the customer can take a 2 percent discount if the invoice is paid in 10 days, but the full amount is due if the invoice is paid in 30 days.

It's also a good idea to specifically state the date the invoice becomes past due to avoid any possible misunderstanding. If you're going to charge a penalty for late payment, be sure your invoice states that it's a late payment or rebilling fee, not a finance charge.

Beware!

If you offer an early-payment discount, be prepared for some customers to deduct the discount but still take 30 days or longer to pay. Some business owners say this is a good reason not to offer such discounts because if you try to collect them when they've been incorrectly taken, you risk damaging your relationship with your customer. It's a judgment call only you can make.

The Taxman Cometh

Businesses are required to pay a wide range of taxes, and there are no exceptions for cleaning service business owners. Keep good records so you can offset your local, state, and federal income taxes with the expenses of operating your company. If you have employees, you'll be responsible for payroll taxes. If you operate as a corporation, you'll have to pay payroll taxes for yourself; as a sole proprietor, you'll pay a self-employment tax. Then there are property taxes; taxes on your equipment and inventory; fees and taxes to maintain your corporate status; your business license fee (which is really a tax); and other lesser-known taxes. Take the time to review all your tax liabilities with your accountant.

Finally, use your invoices as a marketing tool. Mention any upcoming specials, new services, or other information that may encourage your customers to use more of your services. Add a flier or brochure to the envelope—even though the invoice is going to an existing customer, you never know where your brochures will end up.

Establishing Credit Policies

When you extend credit to someone, you're essentially providing them with an interest-free loan. You wouldn't expect someone to lend you money without getting information from you about where you live and work, and your potential ability to repay. It makes sense that you would want to get this information from someone you're lending money to. Reputable companies won't object to providing you with credit information.

Extending credit involves some risk, but it's an essential part of operating successfully, especially if your customer base is primarily other businesses.

Typically, you'll only extend credit to commercial accounts, although some residential cleaning services will extend credit to individuals. But most residential customers will likely pay with cash, check, or a credit card at the time you provide the service. You need to decide how much risk you're willing to take by setting limits on how much credit you'll allow each account.

Your credit policy should include a clear collection strategy. Don't ignore overdue bills; the older a bill gets, the less likely it will ever be paid. Be prepared to take action on past due accounts as soon as they become past due.

Red Flags

Just because a customer passed your first credit check with flying colors, don't neglect to re-evaluate their credit status—in fact, you should do it on a regular basis.

Tell customers when you initially grant their credit applications that you have a policy of periodically reviewing accounts so that when you do it, it's not a surprise. Things can change quickly in the business world, and a company that's on sound financial footing this year may be wobbly next year.

An annual reevaluation of all customers on open accounts is a good idea—but if you start to see trouble in the interim, don't wait to take action. Another time to reevaluate customers' credit is when they request an increase in their credit lines.

Some key trouble signs are a slowdown in payment and difficulty getting answers to your payment inquiries. A sharp increase in complaints could be a red flag; they may be preparing to decline payment based on unsatisfactory service. Also, pay attention to what your customers are doing. A major change in their customer base or product line is something you may want to monitor.

Take the same approach to a credit review that you do to a new credit application. Most of the time, you can use what you have on file to conduct the check, but if you're concerned for any reason, you may want to ask the customer for updated information.

Most customers will understand routine credit reviews and accept them as a sound business practice. A customer who objects may well have something to hide—and that's something you need to know.

Accepting Credit and Debit Cards

Whether your target market is business accounts or individual consumers, it will help if you're able to accept credit and debit cards. Though most businesses prefer to be billed directly for cleaning services, some smaller businesses may want to charge the amount to their company credit card—if for no other reason than to rack up frequent flier miles. And while many consumers will write a check or even pay in cash, a significant number would prefer to use their credit cards—and may even buy more of your services than if they had to pay cash.

Today, it's much easier to get merchant status than it has been in the past because merchant status providers are competing aggressively for your business.

To get a credit card merchant account, start with your own bank. Also check with professional associations that offer merchant status as a member benefit. Shop around; this is a competitive industry, and it's worth taking the time to get the best deal.

The easiest and least expensive way to accept credit cards is by using an online payment service such as PayPal or WePay that allows your clients to pay with their credit cards. The primary drawback is that your clients have to be willing to go online to make their payments (unless you use a mobile app and are face-to-face when you get paid). A benefit is that the money is transferred to your account immediately.

Calculating Markup

Unless you're a mathematics whiz, you may find calculating markup confusing. The following table shows you the percentage you need to mark up your operating costs to reach the desired net profit. Here's how it works: Choose the desired net profit from the left-hand column, then use the markup percent from the corresponding column on the right. For example, if you want a net profit of 4.8 percent, you need to use a markup of 5.01 percent.

Net Profit Percent	Markup Percent	Net Profit Percent Cont'd.	Markup Percent Cont'd.	Net Profit Percent Cont'd.	Markup Percent Cont'd.
4.8	5.01	22.5	29.0	41.0	70.0
5.0	5.3	23.0	29.9	42.0	72.4
6.0	6.4	23.1	30.0	42.8	75.0
7.0	7.5	24.0	31.6	44.4	80.0
8.0	8.7	25.0	33.3	46.1	85.0
9.0	10.0	26.0	35.0	47.5	90.0
10.0	11.1	27.0	37.0	50.0	100
10.7	12.0	27.3	37.5	52.4	110
11.0	12.4	28.0	39.0	54.5	120
11.1	12.5	28.5	40.0	56.5	130
12.0	13.6	29.0	40.9	58.3	140
12.5	14.3	30.0	42.9	60.0	150
13.0	15.0	32.0	47.1	61.5	160
14.0	16.3	33.3	50.0	63.0	170
15.0	17.7	34.0	51.5	64.2	180
16.0	19.1	35.0	53.9	65.5	190
16.7	20.0	35.5	55.0	66.7	200
17.0	20.5	36.0	56.3	69.2	225
18.0	22.0	37.0	58.8	71.4	250
18.5	22.7	37.5	60.0	73.3	275
19.0	23.5	38.0	61.3	75.0	300
20.0	25.0	39.0	64.0	76.4	325
21.0	26.6	39.5	65.5	77.8	350
22.0	28.2	40.0	66.7	78.9	375

Setting Up Your Business

Homebased businesses are common these days, and cleaning services are excellent candidates for this type of setup. After all, your customers will likely never come to your facility since all your work is done on their premises. But that's not the only issue influencing your decision to operate from a homebased office or a commercial location.

Many municipalities have ordinances that limit the nature and volume of commercial activities that can occur in residential areas. Some outright prohibit the establishment of homebased businesses. Others may allow such enterprises but place restrictions regarding issues such as signage, traffic, employees, commercially marked vehicles, and noise. Before you apply for your business license, find out what ordinances govern homebased businesses; you may need to adjust your plan so you comply. If you live in a neighborhood with a homeowners association, you may be subject to additional restrictions; find out what those are before you get too far along in your planning.

Beyond the specific regulations, it's reasonable and fair to operate your business in a manner that won't negatively affect the neighborhood. Be a good citizen, and don't give your neighbors any reason to complain.

Where in your house should your office be? Of course, it's your house—and your decision. When choosing where to set up, first do an analysis of your expected needs and your available space; then try to blend the two. Most cleaning services will need space for two primary functions: administration and storage for equipment and supplies.

It's ideal to locate your business separate from your living area (a spare bedroom is perfect). If that's not possible, you may need to apply some creativity to arranging work areas so they are effective and at the same time don't overtake your personal space. Take the same basic approach to furnishing and equipping your office: Figure out what you need and what you can afford, then begin shopping and setting up.

The Homebased Tax Advantage

Because expenses related to running your business are generally tax-deductible and the IRS has relaxed the rules on what is an allowable home-office deduction, the tax advantage of being homebased is more attractive than ever. The IRS says a home office "will be considered a principal place of business if you perform administrative or management activities there and there is no other fixed location of that trade or business where you conduct substantial administrative or management activities of that trade or business." In other words, even though your actual work will be performed outside your home, your home office will be deductible.

What can you deduct? You can deduct directly related expenses, which are costs that benefit only the business part of your home, as well as a portion of indirect expenses, which are the costs involved in keeping up and running your entire home. For example, your office furniture and equipment are fully deductible and directly related expenses. In the area of indirect expenses, you may deduct a portion of your household utilities and services (electric, gas, water, sewage, trash collection, etc.) based on the percentage of space you use for business purposes. Other examples of indirect expenses include real estate taxes, deductible mortgage interest, casualty losses, rent, insurance, repairs, security systems, and depreciation.

Although you may be concerned that taking the home office deduction will trigger an IRS audit, if your deductions are legitimate and you've kept good records, that shouldn't be an issue. Keep your records for at least three years from the date the return was filed or two years from the date the tax was paid, whichever is later.

> **Tip...**
>
> ## Smart Tip
>
> If you're planning to be homebased and live in an area with extreme temperatures, consider storing your cleaning supplies and chemicals inside your home in a metal storage cabinet so they're protected from excessive heat and cold. In any case, be sure the temperature of the storage area stays within the range recommended by the manufacturers of the products you keep on hand.

The Commercial Option

Many industry veterans believe that to achieve authentic business growth, you must get out of the home and into a commercial facility. Certainly, doing so will help you create a successful and professional image, but before you begin shopping for an office, think carefully about what you'll need.

Your office should be large enough to have a small reception area, work space for yourself and your administrative staff, and a storage area for equipment and supplies. You may also want to have space for a laundry and possibly even a small work area where you can handle minor equipment repairs. Depending on the size of your staff, consider allowing for a small break area, perhaps with lockers for members of your cleaning crews, so they have a place to sit and store personal items when they're in the office at the beginning and end of their shifts.

Regardless of the type of cleaning business you have, remember that chances are slim that your customers will ever come to your office. So look for a facility that meets your operational needs and is in a reasonably safe location, but don't pay for a prestigious address—it's just not worth it.

Vehicles

Because your work is done at your customers' sites, vehicles are important to your business. In fact, your vehicles are essentially your company on wheels. They need to be carefully chosen and well-maintained to adequately serve and represent you.

▲

For a residential cleaning service, an economy car or station wagon should suffice. You need enough room to store equipment and supplies and to transport your cleaning teams, but you typically won't be hauling around pieces of equipment large enough to require a van or small truck.

You can either provide vehicles or have employees use their own. If you provide the vehicles, you can paint your company's name, logo, and telephone number on them. This advertises your business all over town—and especially in the neighborhoods where you're cleaning, since the car will be parked outside your customers' homes while your crews are inside working.

If your employees use their own cars—which is particularly common with residential cleaning services—ask for evidence that they have sufficient insurance to cover them in the event of an accident. Also, confirm with your insurance agent that your own liability policy protects you under those circumstances.

The type of vehicles you'll need for a janitorial service depends on the size and type of equipment you use as well as the size and number of your crews. An economy car or station wagon could work if you're doing relatively light cleaning in smaller offices, but for most janitorial businesses, you're more likely to need a truck or van. A van is preferable over a pickup truck since it allows you to lock your equipment inside, protecting it from theft and the elements. Also, a van painted with your company name, logo, and telephone number will help promote your business.

For carpet cleaning services, you'll need a truck or van, either new or used, for each service person and his or her equipment. A good used truck costs about $10,000 to $12,000, while a new one will run from $19,000 up. You can reduce your startup costs by leasing a truck rather than buying one. There may be other financial and tax benefits to leasing; you need to do an analysis of your situation to make the best decision.

Because your vehicles represent your business, they need to be free of dents and always kept clean, inside and out. This is, after all, a cleaning service—you don't want your customers wondering how good a job you'll do for them if you can't keep your own vehicles clean.

Build a Fleet

When your business grows to the point that you require several vehicles, you can turn to a fleet lessor or dealer program. These programs, designed to help you set up a fleet of commercial vehicles, are run by manufacturers, dealers, leasing companies, and fleet management firms. In the past, only companies with very large fleets could expect special consideration or price breaks on their vehicles. In recent years, vehicle sellers and lessors have recognized the potential market represented by small businesses and have developed fleet programs for companies with as few as three vehicles. It's worth your time to research these programs; you could save lots of money.

Check Out the Drivers

When your employees (or independent contractors) are on the job, you'll likely be liable if an accident occurs while they're driving—whether they're in their own vehicles or yours. Of course, the monetary issues can be handled by insurance—and your insurance agent can help you determine the best types and amounts of coverage to buy—but you'll also want to take steps to prevent problems.

Begin by setting a policy on driver qualifications and history. Be sure anyone driving on company business holds a valid driver's license. Then you need to decide what is and isn't acceptable in the way of violations. A typical policy may be that three or more serious violations (such as reckless driving, speeding 15 miles or more over the speed limit, leaving the scene of an accident, or racing) over a period of two or three years would be cause to reject a prospective job candidate. A drunk driving conviction alone may be reason enough not to hire an applicant who has to drive on the job. You should also look at the individual's accident history. Whatever your policy, apply it consistently to avoid any charge of discrimination.

Drive Safely

Driving a van can be hazardous because the driver sits so close to the front of the vehicle. Also, vans and other marked business vehicles are often the target of scam artists looking to cause a wreck and then file a fraudulent insurance claim. Caution anyone who drives for you on company business—whether in your vehicle or their own—to follow all traffic laws and to leave plenty of space between themselves and the vehicle ahead of them.

▲

When you check references on new employees, ask about their overall dependability and reliability, then find out if they drove a company vehicle in their previous jobs and if they had any driving-related problems.

You may want to require a commercial driver's license. This is more important if the employee will be driving trucks rather than cars. The various classes of commercial licenses vary by state, but they typically require a greater degree of knowledge and experience than a basic operator's license.

Your insurance company may help you develop a policy and screen potential drivers. It's to their benefit, so find out if they'll help you confirm that your employees hold valid licenses and that they have good driving records.

Consider doing an annual review of driving records of all employees who drive on company business. If you see a potential problem, such as a pattern of tickets, you can address it with discipline, training, or even removing the person from their driving position before a situation of serious liability occurs.

Smart Tip

Tip...

Use a street address on your business cards and brochures, even if you operate from home. A street address makes you appear stable and reliable. If your customers mail payments and you wish them to go to a post office box for security reasons, indicate on your invoices that payments should be mailed to a different address. But using a post office box as your primary address makes you look like a temporary, fly-by-night operation, and people might not trust you with cleaning their homes and offices.

Office, Suite Office

You may want to consider setting up your office in an executive suite, where you have access to a range of administrative and support services—such as fax and photocopy machines, and a receptionist—without having to purchase them, and then rent space at a mini-warehouse to store equipment and supplies. The drawback to this, of course, is that you'll have to travel between the two sites.

Human Resources

Although you may eventually be able to operate as an absentee owner, most cleaning service business owners prefer to actively run their businesses. When you're starting out, you'll be wearing a variety of hats, from cleaning technician to salesperson to manager and more. It's not easy, but it will pay off.

You may choose to keep your business small so you can do all the work yourself. This lets you avoid many of the headaches that come with growth and hiring employees. But this isn't a very realistic approach. Operating a cleaning service business is hard enough without complicating it by refusing to recruit employees.

One of the biggest challenges you'll share with businesses in all industries is the demand for qualified workers and rising labor costs. The problem is not so much finding people who can do the work but finding people who want to do the work and who will do it well for wages you can afford to pay.

The first step in a comprehensive human resources program is to decide exactly what you want an employee to do. The job description doesn't have to be as formal as one you might expect from a large corporation, but it needs to clearly outline the person's duties and responsibilities. It should also list any special skills or other required credentials, such as a valid driver's license and clean driving record for someone who's going to be driving a company vehicle.

Next, you need to establish a pay scale. You can do some research on your own to find out what the pay rates are in your area. You'll want to establish a minimum and maximum rate for each position; you'll pay more, even at the start, for better-qualified and more experienced workers.

You'll also need a job application form. You can get a basic form at most office supply stores or you can create your own. In any case, have your attorney review the form you'll be using for compliance with the most current employment laws.

Every prospective employee should fill out an application—even if it's someone you know, and even if they have submitted a detailed resume. A resume isn't a signed, sworn statement acknowledging that you can fire them if they lie; the application is. The application will also help you verify their resumes; compare the two and make sure the information is consistent.

Now you're ready to start looking for candidates.

What Makes a Good Cleaning Service Employee?

What kinds of people make good employees for cleaning service businesses? It depends on what you want them to do. But in general, your ideal employee will enjoy their work and have a great attitude. Certainly they must do a good job, but even if they leave the home or office sparkling, you'll lose business if they're rude to customers. If a cleaner has a poor attitude, chances are they don't truly enjoy the work. And if they don't enjoy the work, it will eventually become evident in the quality of their performance. Look for people who will be enthusiastic about their work and who enjoy cleaning.

Of course, some applicants who love cleaning their own homes may find the reality of cleaning as a job not quite as pleasant. You'll find people who say they love to clean and want to do it for a living, but they don't completely realize that as a job, it's hard work and physically tiring. If you sense a prospective employee feels that they are "above" cleaning for a living, probe further during the interviewing process. If they really feel this way, they may come to work for you because they need a job and the money, but they probably won't stick around very long. Turnover is expensive; it's best to take the time to hire the right people in the first place.

For his St. George, Utah, carpet cleaning business, Mike Blair looks for employees who are personable and have good communication skills. "I call this a white-collar cleaning company—and we do wear white collars—because we require our people to be sharp and reasonably well-educated," he says. "They deal with such a wide variety of situations, and they need to know how to communicate, to ease people's minds, and to develop relationships in addition to simply cleaning."

Look In the Right Places

Picture the ideal candidate in your mind. Is this person likely to be unemployed and reading the classified ads? It's possible, but you'll probably

improve your chances for a successful hire if you're more creative in your searching techniques than simply writing a "help wanted" ad.

Sources for prospective employees include suppliers, customers (use caution here; you don't want to lose a client because you stole an employee), and professional associations. Put the word out among your social contacts as well—you never know who might know the perfect person for your company.

College students make good employees, especially for janitorial services that are often looking for night workers. Students who attend

People Who Need People

Do you need employees to start your cleaning business? Consider these startup staffing suggestions:

For a Residential Cleaning Service

Your initial staffing needs will depend on how much capital you have, how large a business you want to have, and the volume of customers you can reasonably expect to service. Many independent residential cleaning services start with just the owner. Others will start with the owner and an appropriate number of cleaners. If you handle the administrative chores, chances are you won't need to hire office help right away.

For a Janitorial Service

You may be able to start with no employees—or just one or two part-timers. If you have the capital available and the business lined up, you may need to hire more. You may also want to consider an administrative person to handle the records and answer the phone during the day; after all, if you're working all night, you need to schedule some time to sleep. As your business grows, consider a marketing/salesperson, a customer service manager, and crew supervisors as well as additional cleaning personnel.

For a Carpet Cleaning Service

Depending on the strength of your pre-opening campaign and your startup budget, hire at least one service person and possibly two as you're getting started, along with an employee experienced in clerical work who can book appointments and handle administrative chores. Though most residential jobs can likely be handled by one person, you may want to consider staffing each truck with two people: a senior technician and a helper. The helper can assist with the prep work for each job (unloading equipment, moving light furniture, etc.), mix chemicals, empty buckets, clean up afterward, etc. This will make each job go faster, which is more efficient and cost-effective and also generates a greater degree of customer satisfaction.

classes during the day are often available to work for you at night. And if you find them in their freshman and sophomore years, you'll have employees with the potential of working for you for the next three or four years. Residential cleaning services often find that mothers represent a strong pool of candidates, especially those looking to work part time while school is in session.

Consider using a temporary help or employment agency to help you find qualified employees. Many small businesses shy away from agencies because they feel they can't afford the fee—but if the agency handles the advertising, initial screening, and background checks, the fee may be worth paying.

Use caution if you decide to hire friends and relatives—many personal relationships are not strong enough to survive an employee-employer situation. Small-business owners in all industries tell of nightmarish experiences when a friend or relative refused to accept direction or abused a personal relationship in the course of business.

The key to success as an employer is making it clear from the start that you're the one in charge. You don't need to act like a dictator, of course. Be diplomatic, but set the ground rules in advance, and stick to them.

Evaluating Applicants

When you actually begin the hiring process, don't be surprised if you're as nervous at the prospect of interviewing potential employees as they are about being interviewed. They may need a job, but the future of your company is at stake.

It's a good idea to prepare your interview questions in advance. Develop open-ended questions that encourage candidates to talk. In addition to knowing what they've done, you want to find out how they did it. Ask each candidate the same set of questions, and take notes as they respond so you can make an accurate assessment and comparison later.

When the interview is over, let the candidate know what to expect. Is it going to take you several weeks to interview other candidates, check references, and make a decision? Will you want the top candidates to return for a second interview? Will you call the candidate, or should they call you? This is not only a good business practice, but it's also just simple common courtesy.

Always check former employers and personal references. Though many companies are restrictive as to what information they'll verify, you may be surprised at what you can find out. At least confirm that the applicant told the truth about dates and positions held. Personal references are likely to give you some additional insight into the general character and personality of the candidate; this will help you decide if they'll fit into your operation.

Be sure to document every step of the interview and reference-checking process. Even small companies are finding themselves targets of employment discrimination suits; good records are your best defense if it happens to you.

Be particular about whom you hire, even if you're in an area where competition for workers is fierce. A good rule to follow is to only hire people you would trust in your own home—that way, you'll know you can trust them in your customers' homes and

▲

Do You Need a Break?

No matter how much you enjoy your work, you need an occasional break from it. This is a particular challenge for solo operators, but it's critical. You need to be away from your operation occasionally, not only for vacations, but for business reasons, such as attending conferences and trade shows. Also, you need a plan in place in case of illness, accidents, or other emergencies.

If you take a long weekend or just one or two days off, with proper planning, your customers won't even know you were gone. For longer periods away, you have two choices: Ask someone you trust to run the business in your absence, or just close temporarily.

With a staff as your backup, taking a vacation is easier—just be sure your people are well trained and committed to maintaining your service levels when you aren't there.

---

offices. Remember, good employees are the key to happy customers, and happy customers are loyal.

Take Care of Your Employees

Keep in mind that the only thing you have to sell is service, and the only way for your service to be delivered is through your employees. Treat them with respect and let them know you recognize and appreciate their contributions to the company. Pay competitive wages, give increases and bonuses regularly, and always be fair.

Orlando cleaning service operator Wanda Guzman says she worked for an independent cleaning company for a few years before starting her own business. She received no benefits; the company's owner routinely criticized her in front of clients; if a client canceled a cleaning appointment at the last minute, she didn't get paid; and when she left, it had been more than a year and a half since she had received a raise. Now that she's on her own, she makes more money even after factoring in administrative costs. And when she hires people

> **Bright Idea**
> Post the duties of all positions clearly so new people can quickly see what they're supposed to do each day, and also have a clear picture as to how their positions interact with others.

to help her, she treats them with the respect she wanted from her former boss, who did absolutely nothing to earn her loyalty.

A smart strategy is to pay your cleaners slightly more than the going rate in your area. You'll get the best workers, and your turnover will be lower.

Mike Blair pays his carpet cleaning technicians on commission. "We pay them a specific percentage based on their experience and ability," he says. "I think it gives the technician incentive to know that the job is his complete operation. He's responsible for satisfying the customer and making sure the job is done right, all the way to the finish." He says other carpet cleaning companies vary in their compensation plans from the straight commission he pays, to a base salary plus commission, to an hourly rate with no commission.

> **Tip...**
>
> **Smart Tip**
> Be sure your employees are legal. Under federal law, you must verify the identity and employment eligibility of employees; complete and retain the Employment Eligibility Verification Form (I-9) on file for at least three years after the date of hire or one year after employment ends, whichever is longer; and not discriminate on the basis of national origin and citizenship status.

Now That They're Hired

The hiring process is only the beginning of the challenge of having employees. In an ideal world, employees could be hired already knowing everything they need to know. But this isn't an ideal world, and if you want the job done right, you have to teach your people how to do it.

It's likely that the majority of applicants for entry-level cleaning jobs will need training. This isn't necessarily a disadvantage; in fact, you may prefer to handle this yourself since hiring individuals without professional cleaning experience lets you train them to clean your way. Also, training—especially when it's ongoing—is a great tool for building loyalty. When you show your employees that you're willing to invest in them, it helps build a bond that has a positive impact on your service and turnover rates.

Many small businesses conduct their "training" by throwing someone into the job, but that's not fair to the employee, and it's certainly not good for your business. And if you think you can't afford to spend time on training, think again—can you afford *not* to adequately train your employees? Do you really want them interacting with your customers or cleaning homes and offices when you haven't told them how you want things done?

Why Do We Clean?

The reality is that there isn't a lot of prestige associated with working in the cleaning industry, and yet the work itself is extremely important. Teach your employees why doing their jobs well is essential. It's not just to make homes and commercial facilities look nice; it's for public health and a healthy environment, and to protect the building and its contents. The benefits of proper cleaning include:

○ Security, comfort, and productivity in the workplace are increased.
○ Property value is maintained, and the rate of depreciation is reduced.
○ Quality of life is enhanced.
○ Occupants enjoy an elevated sense of well-being and are comfortable reusing space and materials.
○ Waste and hazards are managed, and sanitation is assured.

The amount of training you'll need to do depends largely on the type of cleaning service you have, the equipment your employees use, and what you expect them to do.

Take a positive approach to training. Show your cleaners how to do the job; then, as they begin doing the cleaning themselves, give lots of positive reinforcement for what they're doing well. Rather than harping on the things they're doing wrong, simply show them again how to do those tasks properly.

Blair expects to have to train his carpet cleaning technicians because, he says, finding experienced technicians is rare. "People would be surprised at the level of learning that's required to become a seasoned technician," he says. He sends his new and existing technicians to training programs offered by equipment manufacturers and professional organizations. "It's important to pay the price and get the training," he says.

New technicians begin working with Blair himself or another experienced technician until they know the business well enough to be sent out on their own. Training can take several months, and their first solo job is more likely to be an empty rental than an occupied home or office.

Training Techniques

Whether done in a formal classroom setting or on the job, effective training begins with a clear goal and a plan for reaching it. Training will fall into one of three major categories:

1. orientation, which includes explaining company policies and procedures;
2. job skills, which focuses on how to do specific tasks; and
3. ongoing development, which enhances basic job skills and grooms employees for future challenges and opportunities.

These tips will help you maximize your training efforts:

- *Find out how people learn best.* Delivering training is not a one-size-fits-all proposition. People absorb and process information differently, and your training method needs to be compatible with their individual preferences. Some people can read a manual, others prefer a verbal explanation, and still others need to see a demonstration. In a group training situation, your best strategy is to use a combination of methods; when you're working one-on-one, tailor your delivery to fit the needs of the person you're training.

  With some employees, figuring out how they learn best can be a simple matter of asking them. Others may not be able to tell you because they don't understand it themselves; in those cases, experiment with various training styles and see what works best for the specific employee.

- *Use simulation and role-playing to train, practice, and reinforce.* One of the most effective training techniques is simulation, which involves showing an employee how to do something and then allowing them to practice it in a safe, controlled environment. If the task includes interpersonal skills, let the employee role play with a co-worker to practice what they should say and do in various situations.

- *Be a strong role model.* Don't expect more from your employees than you're willing to do. You're a good role model when you do things the way they should be done all the time. Don't take shortcuts you don't want your employees to take or behave in any way that you don't want them to behave. On the other hand, don't assume that simply doing things the right way is enough to teach others how to do things. Role modeling is not a substitute for training. It reinforces training. If you only role model but never train, employees aren't likely to get the message.

> **Tip...**
>
> **Smart Tip**
>
> Training employees—even part-time, temporary help—to your way of doing things is important. These people represent your company, and they need to know how to maintain the image and standards you've worked hard to establish.

- *Look for training opportunities.* Once you get beyond basic orientation and job skills training, you need to constantly be on the lookout for opportunities to enhance the skills and performance levels of your people.

- *Make it real.* Whenever possible, use real-life situations to train—but avoid letting customers know they've become a training experience for employees.
- *Anticipate questions.* Don't assume that employees know what to ask. In a new situation, people often don't understand enough to formulate questions. Anticipate their questions and answer them in advance.
- *Ask for feedback.* Finally, encourage employees to let you know how you're doing as a trainer. Just as you evaluate their performance, convince them that it's OK to tell you the truth, ask them what they thought of the training and your techniques, and use that information to improve your own skills.

Uniforms

Some cleaning services require their employees to wear uniforms on the job. Uniforms allow customers to identify your workers easily; they also give your operation a professional appearance and advertise your business. Uniforms generally consist of a shirt with your company's name and logo, and comfortable pants that allow employees to bend and stoop easily. You may opt to provide shirts and let your employees wear their own jeans or trousers.

Residential cleaning and janitorial service workers can also benefit from wearing smocks. Smocks with pockets allow your cleaners to carry all their supplies with them—sponges, dust cloths, and spray bottles are always within reach. Not only do smocks save time because cleaners don't have to run around for supplies, but they also keep employees' hands free for cleaning, which means they work more efficiently. Smocks can also protect and prolong the life of a uniform.

Franchises usually sell their franchisees uniforms at discounted prices. A local screen-printing shop can print your company's name and logo on T-shirts for employees to wear as part of their uniforms. You can also check out local uniform shops to see what's available.

If you're going to require your employees to wear uniforms, you should provide at least two or three sets initially and then consider paying a small uniform allowance for maintenance and replacement of garments. How many uniform sets and the amount of the allowance will depend on the cost, durability, and style of the uniform you choose.

Employee Benefits

The wages you pay may be only part of your employees' total compensation. While many very small companies don't offer a formal benefits program, many business owners have recognized that benefits—particularly in the area of insurance—are important in attracting and retaining quality employees.

Typical benefits packages include group insurance (you may need to do some research to determine the impact of Affordable Care Act on your benefits offering), paid holidays, and vacations. You can build employee loyalty by offering additional benefits that may be somewhat unusual—and they don't have to cost much. For example, if you're in or near a retail location, talk to other store owners in your shopping center to see if they're interested in providing your employees with discounts. You'll provide your own employees with a benefit and generate some new customers for your business neighbors.

Beyond tangible benefits, look for ways to provide positive working conditions. Uniforms are one way to create a positive environment. Be sure the equipment and tools you ask your employees to use are in good working condition; substandard supplies can reduce their productivity and their morale. Consider a comfortable break room with adequate lockers and vending machines. You may even want to provide the coffee at no charge. Show your appreciation for jobs well done by paying for lunch (even though "lunch" comes in the middle of the night for third-shift workers); a few pizzas or sandwiches are an inexpensive investment that will pay you back many times over in loyalty and productivity. Insist that everyone in your company, from the most junior part-time cleaner up to and including yourself, be treated and treat others with respect and courtesy at all times—there's just no excuse for operating any other way.

Child Labor Laws

Though teenagers don't make up a significant portion of the cleaning service industry's labor force, it's important that you understand the child labor laws that apply to your operation. Many entrepreneurial cleaning businesses are family-owned, and these owners often employ their kids during summer vacation or for extended periods. The Fair Labor Standards Act has provisions designed to protect the education opportunities of youths and prohibit their employment in jobs and under conditions detrimental to their health and well-being.

The minimum age for most nonfarm work is 16; however, 14- and 15-year-olds may be employed outside of school hours in certain occupations under certain conditions. At any age, youths may work for their parents in their solely owned nonfarm businesses (except in mining, manufacturing, or in any other occupation declared hazardous by the Secretary of Labor); this means your minor children can work in your cleaning service business if you're the sole owner, and as long as you're not violating other age-related laws.

The basic age-related guidelines of the Fair Labor Standards Act are:

- Youths 18 years or older may perform any job for unlimited hours.
- Youths age 16 and 17 may perform any job not declared hazardous by the Secretary of Labor for unlimited hours.
- Youths age 14 and 15 may work outside school hours in various nonmanufacturing, nonmining, nonhazardous jobs under the following conditions: no more than three hours on a school day, 18 hours in a school week, eight hours on a nonschool day, or 40 hours in a nonschool week. In addition, they may not begin work before 7 A.M. nor work after 7 P.M., except from June 1 through Labor Day, when evening work hours are extended to 9 P.M.
- Youths aged 14 and 15 who are enrolled in an approved Work Experience and Career Exploration Program may be employed for up to 23 hours during school weeks and three hours on school days, including during school hours.

Department of Labor regulations require employers to keep records of the dates of birth of employees under age 19, their daily starting and quitting times, daily and weekly hours of work, and their occupations. Protect yourself from unintentional violations of the child labor provisions by keeping on file an employment or

> **Bright Idea**
>
> Give your employees subscriptions to industry trade magazines and newsletters, and encourage them to use and share the information they learn from those publications. The cost is nominal, and the result is that you'll increase their value to the company as well as their sense of self-esteem.

> **Tip...**
>
> **Smart Tip**
>
> From the day they're hired, tell employees what they need to do to get a raise without having to ask for it. Then follow up by increasing their pay rates when they've earned it.

age certificate for each youth employed to show that they're the minimum age for the job.

Keep in mind that, in addition to the federal statutes, most states also have child labor laws. Check with your own state Labor Department to see what state regulations apply to your business. When both the federal law and the state law apply, the law setting the higher standards must be observed.

What Should You Pay?

The Fair Labor Standards Act also establishes minimum wage, overtime pay, and record-keeping standards. The act permits the employment of certain individuals at wage rates below the statutory minimum wage, but they must be working under certificates issued by the Department of Labor. Those individuals include student learners (vocational education students), full-time students in retail or service establishments, and individuals whose earning or productive capacity is impaired by a physical or mental disability, including those related to age or injury. Because laws change, check with your state labor board and/or the U.S. Department of Labor Wage and Hour Division for the current minimum wage amounts.

There's much more involved in setting your wage scales than understanding what the law requires. You must also consider issues such as the skills you require; whether you pay by the hour, by the job, or on a commission basis; whether you offer benefits; whether the people working for you are employees or independent contractors; what the going rates in your area are; and a variety of other factors.

The following are reasonable ranges (you must still study your local market and consider the other factors when setting pay rates). Don't be reluctant to go over these ranges if it's appropriate in your market. If you're in New York City, Chicago, or Los Angeles, for example, you would most likely pay more. The going hourly rate for a residential cleaner is $8 to $12 per hour. For a janitor, it's $8.50 to $12.50 per hour. For a carpet cleaner, hourly wages are approximately $10 to $15 per hour. Keep in mind that the carpet cleaning figure could be less if the worker is also on commission.

Beware!
Employees are sometimes driven to steal because they feel that they're being underpaid or that the business owner is making excessive profits on workers' efforts, so the employee feels "entitled" to steal. Help prevent this attitude by paying fair wages and treating your employees with respect.

Employee Theft

Business owners often work hard to protect their operations from external thieves, without realizing that employees and on-site contract workers actually pose a greater chance of theft. Employee theft can have a serious impact on your bottom line as well as on the morale of other employees who may be aware of what's going on.

As a cleaning service owner, part of the service you offer is trustworthiness, so it's critical that you screen all applicants to reduce the risk that any of your employees will steal either from you or from one of your customers.

Of course, pre-employment screening is just the first step. You should also set policies designed to reduce the opportunity to steal. For example, don't allow employees to take personal items such as purses, bags, or backpacks with them onto the customer's premises. These items can be used to hide stolen items. It's also possible that personal items can get left behind at the customer's site, and retrieving them can be inconvenient for both you and your customer. Prevent either possibility by requiring that all personal belongings be kept locked in the company vehicle or stored in your office in an assigned locker.

Be sure workers are adequately supervised. This not only prevents theft but also assures a quality result. Finally, let there be no misunderstanding about the consequences for stealing, which should be immediate termination.

When You Suspect a Problem

When you become aware of actual or suspected employee theft, you need to act quickly—but carefully—to resolve the situation.

"Treat the complaint as valid until it is established otherwise, and treat the accused as innocent until proven guilty," says Michael P. O'Brien, a labor and employment attorney with Jones Waldo in Salt Lake City. "Also, treat the matter confidentially to the greatest extent possible." In today's litigious world, protecting the privacy of a suspect is essential; failing to do so can leave you vulnerable if that individual decides to sue later on—regardless of whether the person was actually guilty.

The first step is to conduct a thorough investigation, including a review of all relevant documents, such as personnel files, time sheets, performance evaluations of involved persons, inventory and delivery records, and any applicable financial records. If the premises where the theft occurred have a security system that includes video surveillance, you'll want to review the tapes. You may also want to interview witnesses and others who may have knowledge of the situation. Of course, you should also interview the accused—without making an accusation. When conducting interviews, be clear that the issue under investigation isn't to be discussed with unconcerned parties. "If a witness can't be trusted, think carefully about involving that person [in the investigation] in order to avoid possible defamation problems," says O'Brien.

Regardless of how much you trust a particular witness, avoid disclosing information unnecessarily, and don't ask questions that indicate the direction of your inquiry. Document every step of the investigation, and maintain those records in a secure place separate from your personnel records. Don't make details of an investigation part of an employee's personnel file unless and until the results are in and misconduct has been proved.

If your investigation confirms misconduct of any sort, take immediate and appropriate disciplinary action that's consistent with your general policies. "The worst thing you can do is nothing," O'Brien says. "You need to take some sort of disciplinary action against the individual you've concluded has done an inappropriate act." Certainly you'll want to consider the severity, frequency, and pervasiveness of the conduct—for example, occasionally eating candy from the dishes on the desks of your customers' employees is certainly less severe than taking cash or valuable items out of their desks—but whatever remedy you apply must end the offensive behavior. Keep in mind that whatever you do may wind up in court, so maintain good records and be sure you can always justify your actions.

You must also decide whether to involve law enforcement. Weigh the potential for negative publicity against the potential good, which could include restitution and the fact that the perpetrator may receive some much-needed rehabilitation.

Purchasing

When it comes to business purchasing, even the smartest consumer is playing a new game. The rules are different and the stakes significantly higher. But correctly done, purchasing—or procurement—will increase your net income.

Choosing Suppliers

Whether you're buying a major piece of equipment or a bottle of cleaning solution, you should evaluate each vendor on quality, service, and price. Look at the product itself, as well as the supplementary services and support the company provides.

Verify the company's claims before making a purchase commitment. Ask for references, and do a credit check on the vendor just as you would on a new customer. A credit check will tell you how well the supplier pays its own suppliers. This is important because it could ultimately affect you. If your vendor isn't paying his own vendors, he may have trouble getting materials, and that may delay delivery of your order. Or he may simply go out of business without any advance notice, leaving you in the lurch. Also

Bright Idea

Get input from employees when making purchasing decisions on supplies and equipment. The people who are using these items every day know what works and what doesn't, what's efficient and what isn't.

Make a List and Check It Twice

Tracking inventory for a cleaning service business isn't complicated, but it's important. Unlike a retail store, you don't have a wide variety of items to keep up with, but you do need to be sure you have what you need when you need it.

Janitorial services with large buildings as clients usually store products and supplies on site, which means you'll have to track inventory located in multiple sites.

Mike Blair, owner of AAA Prestige Carpet Care in St. George, Utah, says he keeps most of his carpet cleaning supplies on his trucks. "We have shelves on each truck, and we keep a wide variety of chemicals that we utilize in a large variety of situations. It's just a matter of assessing at least once a week what is on the trucks, or having the technicians tell you what they need. I keep [two layers of each item] on the shelf, and when one comes off, I go ahead and order it. We do have a backup inventory, probably another truck's worth, that we keep on the shelves in the storage area. But we don't have to keep a lot of inventory because we can have anything here in two days."

Set up an inventory control and replacement system early and stick with it.

confirm the company's general reputation and financial stability by calling the Better Business Bureau, any appropriate licensing agencies, trade associations, and D&B.

A major component of the purchasing process is the supplier's representative, or salesperson. The knowledge and sophistication levels of individual salespeople often depend on the product or industry; however, they can be a tremendous source of education and information. Make it a rule to treat all salespeople with courtesy and respect.

Besides telling you what they have, salespeople should ask questions. A good salesperson will find out what your needs are and how his company can satisfy them. Just as in the consumer sales arena, commercial salespeople use both high- and low-pressure tactics. Consider studying sales techniques so you can recognize and respond to the methods being used with you.

Buying Supplies

To be sure you don't run out of supplies, you must purchase wisely and in a timely manner. This means establishing and maintaining an effective inventory control system so you'll know when to purchase, what—and what not—to purchase, and how much to purchase. Keep in mind that the caliber of service you provide can be affected by the quality of supplies you use, so choose your products and sources with care.

You probably won't have to use more than a few suppliers to obtain all the supplies you need. Sometimes the suppliers will contact you through their sales reps, but more often, particularly in the beginning, you'll need to locate them. You'll find suppliers of janitorial products in the Yellow Pages of your local telephone directory and by searching online. They also advertise in trade journals and buyers' directories and exhibit at trade shows and conventions. You'll have two basic types of sources: manufacturers and distributors.

You can buy directly from manufacturers through their own salespeople or independent representatives who handle the product lines of several different companies. These sources usually offer the lowest prices but are also likely to have sizable minimum purchase requirements. Also, they may add on the cost of freight, so be sure to get the total price of getting the products to your door before making a buying decision.

You may choose to buy from a distributor, also known as a wholesaler, broker, or jobber.

Dollar Stretcher

It's more cost effective to purchase supplies in bulk rather than in small quantities. You'll also save money by buying larger containers rather than smaller ones.

Sign on the Dotted Line

Contracts are a way to make sure both vendor and customer are clear on the details of the sale. This isn't "just a formality" that can be brushed aside. Read all agreements and support documents carefully, and consider having them reviewed by an attorney. Make sure everything that's important to you is in writing. Remember, if it's not part of the contract, it's not part of the deal—no matter what the salesperson says. And if it's in the contract, it's probably enforceable—even if the salesperson says that never happens.

Any contract the vendor writes is naturally going to favor the vendor, but you don't have to agree to all the standard boilerplate terms. In addition, you can demand the inclusion of details that are appropriate to your specific situation. Consider these points when you're negotiating contracts:

○ *Make standard provisions apply to both parties.* If, for example, the contract exempts the vendor from specific liabilities, request that the language be revised to exempt you, too.

○ *Use precise language.* It's difficult to enforce vague language, so be specific. A clause that states the vendor isn't responsible for failures due to "causes beyond the vendor's control" leaves a lot of room for interpretation; more precise language forces a greater level of accountability.

○ *Include a "vendor default" provision.* The vendor's contract probably describes the circumstances under which you would be considered to be in default; include the same protection for yourself.

○ *Be wary of vendor representatives who have to get any contract changes approved by "corporate" or some other higher authority.* This is a negotiating technique that generally works against the customer. Insist that the vendor make available personnel with the authority to negotiate.

These operators use quantity discounts to buy from various manufacturers, and then warehouse the goods for sale to janitorial services. Although their prices will be higher than if you bought directly from the manufacturer, they can supply you with smaller quantities, which lets you avoid tying up your cash in excess inventory. Typically, they'll be closer to you than the manufacturer, which means quicker delivery time and a lower freight charge. Many manufacturers will only sell to distributors, so if you contact them, they will refer you to a distributor who can work with you.

Dealing with Suppliers

Reliable suppliers are an asset to your business. They can bail you out when you make an ordering mistake or when your clients make difficult demands on you. But they'll do so only as long as your business is profitable to them. Suppliers are in business to make money. If you argue over every invoice, ask them to shave prices on everything they sell you, or fail to pay

> **Bright Idea**
> If your storage space is limited, try negotiating a deal like this: Make a long-term purchase commitment to earn volume pricing, but arrange for delivery in increments so you don't have to store the materials.

your bills promptly, don't be surprised when their salespeople stop calling on you or refuse to help you when you're in a bind.

Of course, you want the best deal you can get on a consistent basis from your suppliers—this is good business. Keep in mind that no worthwhile business arrangement can continue for long unless something of value is rendered and received by all involved. The best approach is to treat your suppliers the way you would like each of your customers to treat you.

Suppliers Are Also Creditors

Most business advice focuses on dealing with your customers, but you're also going to become a customer for your suppliers. That means you'll have to pay for what you buy.

Find out in advance what your suppliers' credit policies are. Most will accept credit cards but will not put you on an open account until they've had a chance to run a check on you. They may ask you to provide a financial statement; if they do, don't even think of inflating your numbers to cover a lack of references. This is a felony, and it's easily detected by most credit managers.

If you do open an account with a supplier, be sure you understand the terms and preserve your credit standing by paying on time. Typically, you'll have 30 days to pay, but many companies offer a discount if you pay early.

Negotiating a Deal

Negotiating doesn't mean that there has to be a winner and a loser. The adversarial relationship that has existed in the past between supplier and customer isn't the best strategy. The most profitable approach is to partner with your suppliers, develop the relationship over time, and work out your differences for a mutual benefit.

The ideal sequence of events in the purchasing process is to determine that the vendor has the product you need, the quality is satisfactory, and the availability in terms of quantity and delivery date meets your requirements. Only then do you begin negotiating price.

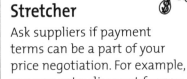

Dollar Stretcher

Ask suppliers if payment terms can be a part of your price negotiation. For example, can you get a discount for paying cash in advance?

Price can be approached from several angles. Consider the cost of the item itself, the quantity discounts, add-ons such as freight and insurance, and the payment terms. To determine the true value of a quantity discount, calculate how long you can expect to have the material or merchandise on hand and what your cost of carrying that inventory is. Payment terms are another important consideration. Some vendors offer substantial discounts for early payment; others will extend what amounts to an interest-free, short-term loan by offering lengthier payment terms.

Of course, price isn't the only negotiable point. Every element of the sale is open for negotiation. At all stages of the process, leave room for some give and take. For example, if you're asking for a lower price or more liberal payment terms, can you agree to a more relaxed delivery schedule?

Young and growing businesses are often at a disadvantage in the negotiating process because their initial volume is small or they don't know what their sales will be. Be honest with vendors. Ask them to take a chance on working with you while you're small, in exchange for future potential. Set a time in the future to analyze how you've done and, if necessary, to renegotiate your terms.

Dollar Stretcher

Purchase used towels in bulk from linen services. Cleaning services will have a variety of uses for towels and other linens that are stained or torn and can no longer be used by the linen services' customers.

The key to successful purchasing is becoming partners with your vendors. Choose them carefully and then nurture your relationships for a mutually rewarding alliance.

Equipment

As you're getting started, you may be focused on buying cleaning equipment—but take your blinders off. You'll also need to stock your office with the equipment and supplies necessary to run your business.

Basic Office Equipment

Many entrepreneurs find a trip to the local office supply store more exciting than any mall. It's easy to get carried away when you're surrounded with an abundance of clever gadgets, all designed to make your working life easier and more fun. But if, like most new business owners, you're starting on a budget, discipline yourself to buy only what you need. Consider these primary basic items:

- *Computer and printer.* A computer can help you manage complex bookkeeping and inventory control tasks, calculate estimates, coordinate work loads, maintain customer records, and produce marketing materials. It's a valuable management and marketing tool, and an essential for growing a strong and profitable business, especially in today's technology-dependent world. Printer technology is advancing rapidly; an office supply dealer can help you decide what type of printer(s) you'll need based on what you expect your output to be.

- *Software.* Think of software as your computer's brains, the instructions that tell your computer how to accomplish the functions you need. There are many programs on the market to handle your accounting, inventory, customer information management, and other administrative tasks. Software can be a significant investment, so do a careful analysis of your needs and then study the market and examine a variety of products before making a final decision.

- *Internet access.* High-speed internet access is essential for an efficient business operation. Your choices will typically include a high-speed telephone line, cable service, wifi, or satellite, although not all these options will be available in every area. The type of equipment you'll need depends on how you'll be accessing the internet, and prices can vary depending on the service you need. Shop around for the best service and price package.

Beware of extremely low prices, as-is deals, and closeouts when it comes to

> ### Beware!
> Although multi-function devices—such as a copier/printer/fax machine or a fax/telephone/answering machine—may cost less initially and need less space in your office than stand–alone items, if the equipment fails, you'll lose all these functions simultaneously. Also, consider the machine's efficiency rating and cost to operate; compare that with stand–alone items before making a purchase. Tough decision? Pick the machine that best suits the needs of your business.

purchasing computer equipment. Deals like these often hide problems you wouldn't want, even for free.

- *Photocopier.* The photocopier is a fixture of the modern office and can be useful to even the smallest cleaning service business. You can get a basic, low-end, no-frills personal copier for $100 to $500 in just about any office supply store. More elaborate models increase proportionately in price. If you anticipate a heavy volume (rare for a cleaning service), consider leasing.

- *Fax machine.* With the ability to easily scan and email documents, the need to send and receive faxes is declining, but you may still want fax capability in your operation. You can either add a fax card to your computer, use an online fax service, or buy a multifunction printer with fax capability or a stand-alone machine. If you use your computer, it must be on to send or receive faxes, and the transmission may interrupt other work. An online fax service will send you an email when you have received a fax. Most residential cleaning operations will have limited fax needs; commercial cleaners will likely have a higher demand for fax service. Expect to pay about $100 for a single-function plain-paper fax machine to $175 to $750 for a multifunction device (fax/copier/printer/scanner).

- *Postage scale.* Unless all your mail is identical, a postage scale is a valuable investment. An accurate scale takes the guesswork out of postage and will quickly pay for itself. It's a good idea to weigh every piece of mail to eliminate the risk of items being returned for insufficient postage or overpaying when you're unsure of the weight. Light mailers—one to 12 articles per day—will be adequately served by inexpensive mechanical postal scales, which typically range from $10 to $25. If you're averaging 12 to 24 items per day, consider a digital scale, which is somewhat more expensive—generally from $50 to $200—but significantly more accurate than a mechanical unit. If you send more than 24 items per day or use priority or expedited services frequently, invest in an electronic computing scale, which weighs the item and calculates the rate via the carrier of your choice, making it easy for you to compare. Programmable electronic scales range from $80 to $250.

- *Postage meter.* Postage meters allow you to pay for postage in advance and print the exact amount on the mailing piece

> **Bright Idea**
>
> Postage stamps come in an array of sizes, designs, and themes, and can add elements of color, whimsy, and even thoughtfulness to mail. Stamps look more personal; metered mail looks more corporate. Consider using metered mail for invoices, statements, and other official business, and stamps for thank-you notes and similar marketing correspondence that could use a personal touch.

when it's used. Many postage meters can print in increments of one-tenth of a cent, which can add up to big savings for bulk mail users. Meters also provide a "big company" professional image, are more convenient than stamps, and can save you money in a number of ways. Postage meters are leased, not sold, with rates starting at about $20 per month, or you can get a meter/electronic scale combo for $30 to $120 per month. They require a license, which is available from your local post office. Only four manu-facturers are licensed by the U.S. Postal Service to manufacture and lease postage meters; your local post office can provide you with contact information. An alternative to a postage meter that will allow you to avoid buying stamps is to print your postage online. Visit the U.S. Postal Service website at usps.gov or check out private companies, such as stamps.com, for more information.

> **Bright Idea**
>
> Be sure to include your area code with your phone number on all your printed materials (stationery, brochures, signs, etc.). As more areas convert to ten-digit dialing with multiple area codes, more consumers will see a seven-digit number as incomplete.

- *Paper shredder.* A response to both a growing concern for privacy and the need to recycle and conserve space in landfills, shredders are increasingly common in both homes and offices. They allow you to destroy incoming unsolicited direct mail, as well as sensitive internal documents before they're discarded. Shredded paper can be compacted more tightly than paper tossed in a waste-basket, so conserves landfill space. Light-duty shredders start at about $25, and heavier-capacity shredders run $150 to $500.

- *Credit- and debit-card processing equipment.* This could range from a mobile device to a simple imprint machine to an online terminal. Consult with several merchant status providers to determine the most appropriate and cost-effective equipment for your business.

Telecommunications

The ability to communicate quickly with your customers and suppliers is essential to any business. Also, being able to reach your employees when they're out on jobs is important. Advancing technology gives you a wide range of telecommunications options. Most telephone companies have created departments dedicated to small and homebased businesses; contact your local service provider and ask to speak with some-one who can review your needs and help you put together a service and equipment pack-age that will work for you. Specific elements to keep in mind include the following.

Telephone

Whether you're homebased or in a commercial location, a single line should be adequate during the startup period. As you grow and your call volume increases, you'll add more lines.

Your telephone can be a tremendous productivity tool, and most of the models on the market today are rich in features you'll find useful. Such features include automatic redial, which redials the last number called at regular intervals until the call is completed; programmable memory for storing frequently called numbers; and speakerphones for hands-free use. You may also want call forwarding, which allows you to forward calls to another number when you're not at your desk, and call waiting, which signals you that another call is coming in while you're on the phone. These services are typically available through your telephone company included in your monthly charge or for a fee.

If you're going to be spending a lot of time on the phone, perhaps doing marketing or handling customer service, consider a headset for comfort and efficiency. A cordless phone lets you move around freely while talking. You may find that this wide variety of products will help you in your business; however, these units vary in price and quality, so research them before making a purchase.

Stock Me Up

In addition to equipment, you'll need an assortment of office supplies. Those items include:

- ❏ Correction fluid or tape (to correct typewritten or hand-written documents)
- ❏ Desktop document trays
- ❏ Letter opener
- ❏ Paper and other supplies for your fax machine (if you have one)
- ❏ Paper clips
- ❏ Pens, pencils, and holders
- ❏ Plain paper and ink and toner for your copier and printer
- ❏ Scissors
- ❏ Scratch pads
- ❏ Staplers, staples, and staple removers
- ❏ "Sticky" notes in an assortment of sizes
- ❏ Tape and dispensers
- ❏ Trash cans

▲

Answering Machine/Voice Mail

Because your business phone should never go unanswered, you need some sort of reliable answering device to take calls when you can't do it yourself. Whether you buy an answering machine (expect to pay $40 to $150 for a model that's suitable for a business) or use the voice-mail service provided through your telephone company depends on your personal preferences, work style, and needs.

Cell Phone

Once considered a luxury, cell phones are as common as land lines and have even replaced land lines for many users. You may want a cell phone that you use exclusively for business so that your staff can reach you at any time. Most have features similar to your office phone—such as caller ID, call waiting, and voice mail—and equipment and service packages are reasonably priced.

Bargain Basement

When you begin shopping for equipment for your cleaning service, keep in mind that you can buy secondhand equipment for a fraction of its retail cost. Businesses that have failed, merged, or outgrown their existing equipment are often good sources for used office equipment. Janitorial and residential cleaning companies can be sources of used cleaning equipment, and carpet cleaning businesses may be selling their used carpet cleaning equipment.

Judicious shopping can turn up some excellent bargains. Check the classified section of your daily paper and the weekly business journal for furniture and equipment bargains. Also check the "Business Opportunities" or "Businesses for Sale" categories—businesses that are being liquidated or sold may have excess furniture or equipment for sale at substantial savings. Check eBay and other online auctions, as well as online classified sites such as Craigslist, for new, used, and reconditioned equipment.

Another good source for used equipment is new equipment suppliers. They frequently have trade-ins or repossessions for 50 percent off. Often, these items have been refurbished and even include a warranty.

Toll-Free Number

Most cleaning services are local operations. But if you're planning to build a large operation, or if you're in a niche business and targeting a customer base outside your local calling area, you'll want to provide a toll-free number. This way, customers who don't have free or flat-rate long-distance can reach you without having to make a toll call. Most long-distance service providers offer toll-free numbers, and they have a wide range of service and price packages. If you have a regional business, you may also find a toll-free number useful. Shop around to find the best deal for you.

Email

Email is a standard element in any company's communication package. It allows for fast, efficient, 24-hour communication. Using an email address with your company's website instead of a general provider like AOL, Yahoo!, or Google makes you look more professional. Check your messages regularly and reply to them promptly. Email costs range from free to $20 per month.

Dollar Stretcher

When a postage increase is coming up, stock up on "forever" stamps, which can be purchased at the current rate and are good for mailing one–ounce first-class mail anytime in the future, regardless of price changes.

The Best Equipment Is Information

One of the most efficient and effective ways to promote any business is through content marketing, defined by the Content Marketing Institute as "a marketing technique of creating and distributing relevant and valuable content to attract, acquire, and engage a clearly defined and understood target audience—with the objective of driving profitable customer action." The idea is to provide information that has value to your audience through your online content. You can share and promote that content through a variety of ways, and one of the most popular is social marketing. But if you're going to do it, you need to do it right.

The two primary components of social marketing are media and networking. Social media are websites and applications used for social networking. Social networking is the use of dedicated websites and applications to communicate informally with other users or to find people with similar interests to oneself.

Perhaps the biggest challenge of social marketing is the number of platforms available and the rapidly-changing popularity of those platforms, which is why we're not going to give you how-to lessons on specific social media sites. It's not necessary for you and your company to be active on every social network. A smarter strategy is to pick the two or three networks that are most popular with your market and establish your presence on them, and not worry about the others.

It's important to keep in mind that social marketing should be only one component of your overall marketing strategy. You've probably heard plenty of stories about companies that have thousands or even millions of fans and followers, and thought that you should try to do the same. The reality is that you should do what's best for your company and what matches your strategy. These steps will help you get started:

1. *Set clear goals for your social marketing efforts.* Be specific and keep those goals in mind with everything you do.

2. *Dedicate the human resources to social marketing.* You need someone on your team (and it could be you) who understands social marketing, is comfortable with the platforms you'll be using, and has the time to manage your social marketing program.

3. *Be prepared to produce sufficient content.* Content is the fuel for your social marketing vehicle, and without it, your efforts will stall.

> **Stat Fact**
> Of marketers surveyed by Social Media Examiner, 89 percent said that increased exposure was the number-one benefit of social media marketing.

4. *Prepare your website for social media attention.* Be sure your website is ready for the increased traffic social marketing could generate.

5. *Remember that it's a conversation.* Don't simply talk at your audience, engage with them.

6. *Create a social media policy for your employees.* Employees need to know what they can—and can't—say about the company when they are online.

7. *Be realistic in your expectations.* Don't anticipate monumental results for a minimal investment.

In the next chapter, we'll discuss how to create a complete marketing plan for your cleaning service business.

Marketing

f you've built the proverbial better mousetrap, will the world really beat a path to your door? Only if they know about your business. Of course, you must provide quality service, but you must also create a marketing machine to help drive your sales. Check out *Start Your Own Business* (Entrepreneur Press), which explains how to create a basic marketing plan, but

▲

there are issues and ideas specific to the cleaning service business that you need to know as you develop your plan.

Researching and Defining Your Market

Though the total market for cleaning services is tremendous, you must decide on the particular niche you'll target. If you want to do residential cleaning, do you want to clean private homes, condos and apartments, or empty rental units? If you're starting a janitorial business, will you focus on offices, retail operations, or manufacturing facilities? And will you target small, medium, or large customers? As a carpet cleaner, will you clean residential or commercial facilities—or both? And what services other than shampooing carpets will you provide?

Once you've decided on a market niche, you must look at the geographic area you want to serve. If you're starting a residential cleaning service, as we discussed in Chapter 3, you want to be able to schedule cleanings in a way that minimizes your travel time, so you need to restrict your service area to a particular part of town. The same applies to carpet cleaners. Janitorial crews that must move from building to building have a similar concern.

Talk of the Town

Aprospective customer begins forming an opinion of your operation from the moment your phone is—or isn't—answered. Handling incoming calls should be an important part of your marketing strategy. Regardless of the size of your company and whether you answer incoming calls yourself or have a receptionist, consider these suggestions:

○ Answer all calls promptly; a good goal is by the second ring.
○ Speak clearly and distinctly so there is no doubt as to what company the caller has reached.
○ Give the name of the company, the individual's name, and then offer to help. For example: "Good morning, ABC Cleaning. This is Julie. How may I help you?"
○ Always get permission before placing a call on hold.
○ Use a warm, friendly tone; smile at callers even though they can't see you.

After you've identified what you want to do and where you'd like to do it, research the demographics of the area to be sure it contains a sufficient number of potential customers. If it does, you're ready to move ahead. If it doesn't, you'll need to reconsider how you've defined your niche or the geographic area.

Your market research doesn't have to be extremely sophisticated. Many small residential cleaning service owners simply talk to their friends. Carpet and upholstery cleaning service owner Mike Blair began by talking with people he knew in the St. George, Utah, community. When they indicated there was room for another quality cleaner, he checked the Yellow Pages to identify how many companies he would be competing with, did some basic demographic analysis, and got to work.

> **Tip...**
>
> **Smart Tip**
> Once you're established, be sure to use your longevity as a marketing tool. Because many cleaning service businesses require a minimal investment and are easy to start, the attrition rate is high. Customers prefer to do business with companies they believe will be around in the future, so after you've been in business a few years, trumpet that fact in your marketing efforts.

Part of your market analysis includes your costs to serve that market. A densely populated market allows you to serve a greater number of customers because your travel time is minimal, but it also means you'll be consuming more supplies. This needs to be planned for as well as factored into your rates.

You can build a successful cleaning business based on referrals, but you need those first customers to get started. Where are they? Indianapolis-based Bane-Clene Corp. suggests you start by contacting the following groups:

- Friends and relatives
- Neighbors
- Former co-workers and employers
- Social groups and clubs, including card clubs, bowling teams, athletic leagues, lodges, fraternities, alumni groups, and neighborhood associations
- Church or religious acquaintances

Communicating with Your Market

Communicating with your market to encourage people to become customers is known as marketing. Marketing isn't an exact science, and what works for one company may not work for another. Even so, the best approach is to look at what other successful companies are doing and adapt their techniques to your operation. Give each marketing effort a reasonable chance to work, but if you aren't getting an adequate return on your investment, try something else.

Most of your marketing efforts will cost money, which is why you need to be able to measure the results of the campaigns. You don't want to keep spending money on an advertising program that isn't working, and when you find something that's successful, you'll probably want to do more of it. If you use coupons, you can code them. When new customers call, ask how they heard about you. If it was from an ad, find out which one. If it was a referral, get the name of the person who recommended you.

Networking is one of the most difficult marketing efforts to measure. It won't be exact, but

> **Smart Tip** Tip...
>
> Ask every new customer how they found out about you. Make a note of where they heard about you and what kind of business they represent. This will tell you how well your various marketing efforts are working. You can then decide to increase certain programs and eliminate those that either aren't working or are attracting a type of business you don't want.

you should keep track of how much time you spend on various networking efforts and how much business you credit to those contacts so you can be sure your time is well spent.

Carpet and upholstery cleaner Blair says he invests 5 to 8 percent of his gross profit in marketing. "We do coupons, radio ads, and some television and print media," he says. "Then we call our customers back after the job is done and let them know we're grateful for their business and make sure the work was done to their liking. If we can't reach them by phone, we send a personal note."

Wherever you place it, your marketing message should contain these basic elements:

- What you do
- The benefit the customer will receive when they buy your service
- Who you are
- How to reach you

Here is what some successful cleaning business owners do to market their companies:

- *Make customer service a marketing tool.* There is probably no business where customer service works better as a marketing tool than in the cleaning business. You'll have a lot of opportunity to interact with your customers; take advantage of each contact to demonstrate your superior service.
- *Make people want to talk about you in a positive way.* Word-of-mouth is absolutely the best advertising—and it's free. If you do a great job, your customers will tell their friends and associates. (Of course, they'll also tell their friends and associates if you do a bad job!) Especially if you're small and want to stay that way, word-of-mouth may be your primary method of advertising. Orlando

▲

Dead as a Doorknob

Many cleaning services that target residential customers use doorknob hangers to let neighbors know they've done a job in the area. While this may generate some new business for you, it's an approach that could backfire.

When the service subsidiary of Indianapolis–based Bane–Clene Corp. conducted a survey on the issue, they found that the majority of consumers don't wish to be used as referrals unless they decide to do the referring themselves. Another objection to doorknob hangers is that if the resident is out of town, your sales piece becomes an alert to burglars that no one is at home.

Bane–Clene advises limiting your use of doorknob hangers to serving as a notice of your visit and instructions for rescheduling if the customer isn't at home at the time of your appointment.

maid service owner Fenna Owens says, "I've never advertised because other people refer me."

- *Reward referrals.* An existing customer who refers a new customer should at the very least be thanked, and at the most receive some sort of compensation or reward. An important point to keep in mind about referrals is that people rarely make a referral because you're going to give them something. They make referrals because they like what you do, they believe you'll do a good job for the other person, and when you do, you make them look like stars because they were smart enough to know you. But a referral reward of some sort is a way to emphasize to your existing customers how important referrals are to you.

- *Make yourself visible.* One of the simplest ways to build business and set yourself apart from the competition is to just get out there and be visible. Knock on doors, hand out brochures, go to networking events—do whatever it takes to make sure people know about your company and understand what you do.

> **Bright Idea**
>
> If you operate a residential cleaning business, offer gift certificates so your services can be purchased as a gift. People will give one–time–only cleanings to friends and relatives for special occasions, before holidays, or to help out during a crisis. This will not only generate extra revenue for you, but the recipients of the gift may become customers.

- *Get professional help.* Your marketing materials project the image of your company—and if you want to be perceived as a professional operation, your marketing materials need to look professional. Just because you have a computer and a laser printer doesn't mean you can turn out quality ads and brochures.

If you can't afford to hire an ad agency, look for less expensive alternatives. Blair suggests checking with the marketing department at your local college or university. Students will often take on your business as a project at no cost (or a nominal fee for materials) and help you develop a marketing plan and professionally designed collateral material.

> **Bright Idea**
>
> Human nature mandates that people will go to greater lengths to avoid pain than they will to seek pleasure. As you develop your marketing plan, focus on communicating the message that you can help your customers avoid the pain of doing the cleaning themselves.

Another thing you may want to consider is joining a lead-exchange club to kick start your referrals. Most of these clubs are groups of local business owners, professionals, and salespeople who want to build their customer base. Typically, they restrict membership to one person in a given industry, so you won't have any competitors in the group. They meet regularly—weekly, biweekly, or monthly—and each member is expected to bring at least one lead to the meeting. The lead can be for any other member or for the group at large. Members of these groups usually become each other's customers as well.

To find a lead-exchange group, check the business calendar section of your local paper or an online resource such as Meetup.com; many groups post notices of their meetings and will have a number you can call for more information. Check out several before deciding which one to join; make sure the group you choose is dynamic and will generate some good leads for you.

What About Your Website?

In the internet age, every business should have an online presence, even if it's only a basic website. If you're starting a janitorial or other cleaning service that targets business customers, a website is important because it helps establish you as a legitimate, credible company. If you're planning to be a small, one- or two-person operation targeting residential clients, you can probably get by without a site. Of course, if you're going to accept online payments through a service such as PayPal, a website is essential.

A website will allow prospective customers to learn more about you before they call. You can include the services you offer, the geographical area you serve, and contact information, and have a form that will let visitors ask questions or request a quote. Your site should be professionally designed, user-friendly, and always up-to-date.

The Elements of Image

One of your most important marketing tools is the image you project. Jim Cavanaugh, founder of Jani-King International, a commercial cleaning franchise in Dallas, says image is made up of several components, including:

- *The way you and your crew look.* Are your workers clean and neat, wearing attractive uniforms or at least nice jeans or slacks?

- *Your printed materials.* Are your invoices and statements typed neatly or computerized? Do the documents you produce display professionalism, or do you damage your image by using handwritten bills and scrap paper for notes?

- *Equipment.* Is your equipment clean and in good repair, or dirty, with loose wheels, taped cords, and in general disrepair?

- *Integrity.* Do you operate and behave in such a way that building managers and owners are comfortable trusting you and your employees with unsupervised access to their facilities?

- *Insurance.* Having adequate business insurance, including liability, workers' compensation, and bonding your employees, builds your credibility and image.

- *Your vehicles.* Are your company vehicles clean, running properly, and neatly marked with your company name and logo? A dirty, dented truck that belches smoke won't impress your clients.

You can create a positive image for your company by getting involved in a community service program. In 1996, Ann Arbor, Michigan-based Molly Maid, a residential cleaning franchise, established its Ms. Molly Foundation, which holds an annual "Making a Difference" drive to assist victims of domestic violence. The foundation was established to provide financial and in-kind support to safe houses and shelters, as well as promote education on issues related to domestic violence, including the dynamics involved, safety tips, and escape planning.

Each year in October, Domestic Violence Awareness Month, Molly Maid's home service professionals place a small card in the home of each customer explaining the mission of the Ms. Molly Foundation. This offers the customer an opportunity to participate by donating needed items to shelters. The program lets Molly Maid's home service workers, many of whom are unable to make sizable cash donations, contribute meaningfully to a cause that's important to them. It also boosts the company's image with its current customers as well as within the community at large.

You may not be in a position to form your own nonprofit foundation, but you can easily do small-scale activities, such as sponsoring teams in fund-raising walks, making a contribution to a charity as a referral reward, or donating a few hours of your cleaning services to a worthy cause.

Trade Shows

Trade shows can be a tremendous source of education and information about the cleaning industry, and they can also be a great way to market. Blair attended a number of trade shows, especially when he was new to the business. "They were very beneficial, and I highly recommend trade shows as a way to shop," he says. But when you're at a show, don't just shop.

In addition to attending trade shows to find equipment and supplies and learn more about running your business, consider exhibiting at trade shows to market your services. Local trade shows can provide a tremendous amount of exposure at a very affordable cost.

There are two types of shows—consumer (which focus on home, garden, and other consumer themes) and business-to-business (where exhibitors market their products and services to other companies). Which will work best for you depends on the type of cleaning business you have and the market you're targeting.

"When you go to a show, you're tapping into an audience that is typically outside your network," says Allen Konopacki, a trade show consultant with Incomm Research Center in Chicago. "The other important thing is that the individuals who are going to shows are usually driven by a need. In fact, 76 percent of the people who go to a show are looking to make some kind of a decision on a purchase in the near future."

To find out about shows in your area, call your local chamber of commerce or convention center and ask for a calendar. You can also check out *Trade Show Week Show Directory*, which should be available in your public library, or do an internet search.

When you have identified potential shows, contact the sponsor for details. Find out who will attend—show sponsors should be able to estimate the total attendance and give you demographics so you can tell if the attendees fit your target market profile.

Trade Secrets

Trade shows and conventions are valuable business tools, whether you're attending to shop and learn or exhibiting to get more business. For more information on how to get more out of trade shows, and to find show schedules, visit these trade show websites: Expo Central International, expocentral.com; Incomm Research Center, tradeshowresearch.com; and Trade Show News Network, tsnn.com.

Also ask if it's appropriate to make sales from your booth so you can plan your display and bring sufficient inventory.

Give as much thought to the setup of your booth as you would to an in-store display. Your exhibit doesn't need to be elaborate or expensive, but it does need to be professional and inviting. Avoid trying to cram so much into your booth that it looks cluttered.

Your signage should focus first on the problems you solve for clients and then list your company name. If you have a maid service, one of the major benefits you provide to customers is giving them some free time. So your sign might read:

> **Spend Saturdays doing what you want.**
> **We'll clean your house**
> **so you don't have to.**
> **ABC Maid Service**

Although the show sponsors will probably provide one, don't put a table across the front of your exhibit space; that creates a visual and psychological barrier and will discourage visitors from coming in.

Don't leave your booth unattended during exhibit hours. First, it's a security risk—at a busy show, it would be easy for someone to walk off with valuable equipment. More important, you could miss a tremendous sales opportunity. Even if you're a one-person operation, find someone who can work the show with you so that you can take breaks during the day.

Consider some sort of giveaway items such as pens, mugs, or notepads imprinted with your company name. But, says Konopacki, don't display these items openly; that will only crowd your booth with "trade show tourists." Instead, store them discreetly out of sight and present them individually as appropriate. You should also have a stock of brochures, business cards, and perhaps discount coupons.

To collect lead information for later follow-up, consider giving away a reasonable amount of your services. If you have a maid service, you could give away a certificate worth three hours of cleaning time. A carpet cleaner could give away cleaning three rooms of carpet, or one room and two pieces of upholstered furniture. Hold a drawing that people must register for, and make the registration form a lead qualification tool. For example, if it's a business-to-business show, the registration form should ask their name, company name, whether an outside janitorial service is used, who in the company should be contacted to learn more about what you have to offer, and, of course, complete address and telephone and email information. At a consumer show, find out if they live in apartments, condos, or single-family homes, if they own or rent, and get contact information. Depending on the size and duration of the show,

▲

consider giving away more than one service package so you can hold drawings several times during the course of the show.

When the show is over, immediately send a follow-up letter either via email or regular mail to all the qualified leads you collected, thanking them for visiting your booth and reminding them of the services you offer. Don't assume that they'll keep the information they picked up at the show; chances are, it will be lost in the pile of material from other exhibitors.

Trade Show Tips

A carnival-like atmosphere permeates many trade shows. You want all involved to enjoy themselves, but remember this is a business occasion. Your booth is your store/office for the duration of the show, and it should be a place where you're proud to meet with customers. Establishing dress and conduct rules for your booth staff will make your trade show experience much more rewarding.

- *No smoking, drinking, eating, or gum-chewing by booth staffers.* Too many people are offended by cigarette smoke, and most exhibit halls restrict smoking to designated areas. While most shows provide refreshments, bringing food and beverages into the booth creates an unattractive mess. Who wants to talk to a sales rep whose mouth is full?

- *Dress appropriately.* Just because the show is taking place in a resort doesn't mean you should wear shorts. Standard business attire and comfortable shoes are the best bet.

- *Staff the booth properly.* Two people for every ten feet of space is a good rule of thumb. The key is to make sure your booth isn't overcrowded with your own people or understaffed so visitors can't get the assistance they need.

- *Take regular breaks.* Trade shows can be exhausting. Plan to allow everyone a few minutes away from the booth at scheduled intervals. Also allow time for personnel to see the entire show as early as possible; they'll gain a feel for the competition and pick up ideas for your next show.

- *Remain standing.* Talk to each other only when necessary. Potential visitors may be reluctant to approach your booth if it appears that your salespeople are just relaxing and having a great time chatting among themselves.

> ## Tip...
> **Smart Tip**
> When you hand someone your business card, always give them two—one for them to keep and one for them to pass on to someone else.

Tales from the Trenches

By now, you should know how to get started and you have a good idea of what to do—and not to do—in your own cleaning service business. But nothing teaches as well as the voice of experience. So we asked established cleaning service business operators to tell us what has contributed to their success and what they think causes some companies to fail. Here are their stories.

Never Stop Learning

The cleaning industry may not be the most glamorous or complex, but established business owners say there's always something to learn. Technology advances affect the equipment you use, safety issues affect the chemicals you clean with, and there will always be ways you can enhance your organizational and managerial skills.

Read industry publications, go to meetings and conventions, participate in trade organizations, and encourage your suppliers to keep you up to date.

Tap All Your Resources

A wide range of associations serves various aspects of the professional cleaning industry. These groups can help you with operational, marketing, and management issues. Many state and government agencies also offer support and information for small businesses. Salt Lake City janitorial service owner Michael Ray says using professional associations and seeking help from the government are great ways to maximize your resources.

Clean It Like It's Your Own

Regardless of what you're cleaning and whether you're doing traditional housecleaning or janitorial work, or providing a specialty cleaning service, clean like you're cleaning your own home or office. Residential cleaning service owner Fenna Owens in Orlando has a waiting list of people who want to hire her because, she says, "I do what I would like to have done at my house."

Develop Systems

Systems provide a structure that allows you to work consistently and efficiently, and also let you create a company that will continue to run whether you're there or not. Ray has created systems for every function: cleaning, laundry, supervision, reporting, customer service, accounting, and management.

Be Careful!

Though time is your most valuable commodity, don't rush so much that you get careless. Owens once accidentally vacuumed up some computer wires; fortunately, the replacement part only cost $70 (it could have been substantially more). More important, the customer wasn't happy.

Customers will usually understand that accidents happen, but you're better off if you don't have to fall back on that. Also, the cost to repair or replace something—in out-of-pocket cash, time lost, and damaged customer relations—is usually far more than the time you might save by working carelessly.

Don't Undersell Yourself

When you're starting out, you may be tempted to try to undercut the competition's prices. A better strategy is to simply outperform them by providing quality work.

"When I first started, if somebody was charging $50, I would do it for $40," Owens says. Now she quotes strictly on the amount of work involved. "If you're good, people will pay you—and they'll see within one week whether you're good or not."

Take Care of Your Employees

Your employees are critical to your success; after all, it's the quality of their performance that determines whether your customers are satisfied. Look for ways to make them want to do their best. Train them well, don't micromanage, and treat them with respect. Provide bonuses and incentives for top performance, and consider offering perks such as letting your employees use company equipment in their own homes.

Prepare for the Worst

No matter how knowledgeable or skilled you are, you'll always have problems, and you need to be prepared to deal with them. "There is never a day when you would say everything is perfect," Ray says. "Today, I'm not asking *if* there are problems in my company, I'm asking *where* they are. I can go to any building and find some problems. It's a humbling thing, because there is always something around the corner that needs to be addressed."

Watch Your Chemical Combos

Be careful not to mix cleaning solutions except as suggested by the manufacturer; you could inadvertently create a dangerous compound. Owens learned that the hard way when she followed a customer's request to use a particular chemical combination—which created fumes that caused Owens and her customer to flee the house, gasping for air.

Find a Niche

Don't try to be all things to all people; pick the market you can best serve, and focus on that. For example, Ray's janitorial service market consists of office buildings, manufacturing plants, and corporate headquarters that are more than 100,000 square feet. Because a supervisor is assigned to each work site, Ray's company can't provide quality work at a profitable price level to smaller facilities. "Excel in what you're doing and build consistency in the services you provide," he says. When you try to serve too many markets, you won't be successful in any of them.

Develop Your Computer Skills

You need to be as skilled with your computer as you are with a mop or buffer. The cleaning business may not be particularly high tech, but you don't have time to do estimates, billing, payroll, inventory control, and other record-keeping by hand.

Ray recommends using a spreadsheet program to calculate the workload for janitorial jobs. "You owe it to yourself to get familiar with a spreadsheet program," he says. "You can use it for so many things."

Track Labor Costs

The biggest single expense you have is labor, and you must stay on top of it. "If you are not watching your labor costs every day, it will get away from you like a two-year-old left alone in the kitchen," says Ray. "Work fills the time allowed for its completion. Watch your labor every day. Make sure it's within your budget. We have a daily over and under report, which is one of our most effective tools." The report makes it easy to spot trends before they become major issues.

If labor is on the increase, figure out where the problem is. Is the customer asking for extra services you aren't charging for? Did you underestimate the time it would take to do the work? If you're under on your labor estimates, make sure your employees are providing the quality you've promised.

Invest in Customer Service

The quality of your cleaning is important, but it's not everything. Building strong relationships with your clients requires a serious commitment to customer service. Don't assume that just because the work looks satisfactory to you that it is to your customers—or that there's nothing else they want or need.

Ray has a full-time customer service manager. "His full-time job is to go out to our buildings and talk to the customers, inspect their facilities, make sure they're happy, make sure they know we're interested, that we care, that we want to know how things are going," he says. "Most companies have somebody in management who doubles as that and goes out to talk to customers when there's a problem. But we have somebody who's proactive. He does a written report on every building, and the customer gets a copy of that report. They see what we see as problems and our plans for improvement."

Keep Your Eye on the Economy

As long as things get dirty, there will be a need for professionals to clean them. But economic changes can mean changes in your market. Residential cleaning services, for example, are often seen as luxuries, and an economic downturn could affect your customers' willingness and ability to pay to have their homes cleaned. When business profits shrink, companies look for ways to cut expenses, which means they may examine their cleaning budgets for services that can be reduced or eliminated.

Also consider how the world economy can impact your profitability. If oil prices skyrocket, you'll have to spend more to operate your vehicles, and your general utility costs will probably increase. When the cost of lumber goes up, so does the cost of bathroom tissue, paper towels, and other disposable paper products you provide to your customers. You may be able to pass along some of those costs, but don't let that be your only strategy for dealing with such occurrences.

Don't depend on a thriving economy to keep your business profitable. Have plans in place so you can shift your market focus if necessary. You may want to target a different group of customers or adjust your service offerings and pricing. Don't invest a great deal of time on this issue too far in advance, but be prepared to deal with it if it becomes necessary.

Don't Take Every Job

If you can't make money on a job, or if the work is undesirable for any reason, turn it down. It's better to focus your time and energy on profitable work you enjoy.

Appendix
Cleaning Services
Resources

They say you can never be too rich or too thin. While these could be argued, we believe you can never have too many resources. Therefore, we present for your consideration a wealth of sources for you to check into, check out, and harness for your own personal information blitz. These sources are tidbits, ideas to get you started on your research.

They are by no means the only sources out there, and they shouldn't be taken as the Ultimate Answer. We have done our research, but businesses tend to move, change, fold, and expand. As we have repeatedly stressed, do your homework. Get out there and start investigating.

Associations

Association of Residential Cleaning Services International
7870 Olentangy River Rd., #300
Columbus, OH 43235
(614) 547-0887
arcsi.org

▲

Building Service Contractors Association International
330 N. Wabash Ave., Suite 2000
Chicago, IL 60611
(800) 368-3414, (312) 321-5167
bscai.org

Carpet and Rug Institute
P.O. Box 2048
Dalton, GA 30722-2048
(706) 278-3176
carpet-rug.org

Carpet Cleaners Institute of the Northwest
Association Management Inc.
PMB 366, 2661 N. Pearl
Tacoma, WA 98407
(877) 692-2469, (253) 265-3042
ccinw.org

Chimney Safety Institute of America
2155 Commercial Dr.
Plainfield, IN 46168
(317) 837-5362
csia.org

Cleaning Equipment Trade Association
P.O. Box 1710
Indian Trail, NC 28079
(800) 441-0111, (704) 635-7362
ceta.org

Cleaning Management Institute
cminstitute.net

Institute of Inspection, Cleaning and Restoration Certification
2515 E. Mill Plain Bl.
Vancouver, WA 98661
(360) 693-5675
iicrc.org

International Janitorial Cleaning Services Association
2011 Oak
Wyandotte, MI 48192
(734) 252-6189
ijcsa.com

International Window Cleaning Association
1100-H Brandywine Blvd.
Zanesville, OH 43701
(800) 875-4922
iwca.org

ISSA: The Worldwide Cleaning Industry Association
7373 N. Lincoln Ave.
Lincolnwood, IL 60712-1799
(800) 225-4772, (847) 982-0800
issa.com

Professional Association of Cleaning and Restoration
P.O. Box 21412
Denver, CO 80221
(877) 447-2822
professionalassociationofcleaningandrestoration.org

Restoration Industry Association
12339 Carroll Ave.
Rockville, MD 20852
(301) 231-6505
restorationindustry.org

Society of Cleaning and Restoration Technicians
4402 S. Danville Dr.
Abilene, TX 79605
(800) 949-4728
scrt.org

Consultants and Other Experts

David Cohen
President, Benchmark Logistics Group Inc.
945 Clint Moore Rd.
Boca Raton, FL 33487
(561) 852-1099
benchmarklg.com

Sharon L. Cowan, CBSE
Cleaning Business Consulting Group
2125 82nd Ave.,, S.W.

Vero Beach, FL 32968
(772) 563-7320
cleaningbusinessconsultinggroup.com

Allen Konopacki
Trade Show Consultant
Incomm Research Center
5574 N. Northwest Hwy.
Chicago, IL 60630
(312) 642-9377
tradeshowresearch.com

Patti Page
pagespersonalcleaning.net

Credit Card Services

American Express Merchant Services
(888) 829-7302
merchant.americanexpress.com

Discover Card Merchant Services
(800) 347-6673
discovernewtwork.com/merchants

Master Card
mastercard.com/merchants

PayPal
paypal.com

VISA
usa.visa.com/merchants

WePay
wepay.com

Equipment and Supply Sources

Bane-Clene Corp.
Carpet and floor cleaning equipment supplies, training, and services

3940 N. Keystone Ave.
Indianapolis, IN 46205
(800) 428-9512, (317) 546-5448
baneclene.com

DirtyBlinds.com
Blind cleaners and light lens cleaners
11256 Broadway
Alden, NY 14004
(800) 976-6427, (716) 685-9203
dirtyblinds.com

Industrial Supply
Safety equipment, cleaning equipment, and supplies
1635 South 300 West
Salt Lake City, UT 84115
(801) 484-8644
indsupply.com

International Ceiling and Wall Cleaning Inc.
Ceiling and wall cleaning products and equipment
1555 Sunshine Dr.
Clearwater, FL 33765
(800) 628-4422
icwc.com

J. Racenstein & Co. Inc.
Window cleaning tools and equipment
74 Henry St.
Secaucus, NJ 07094
(800) 221-3748
jracenstein.com

Powr-Flite
Commercial floor care equipment
3101 Wichita Ct.
Fort Worth, TX 76140-1710
(800) 880-2913, (817) 551-0700
powr-flite.com

Pro-Team
Backpack vacuums
(866) 888-2168
pro-team.com

Royce Rolls Ringer Co.
Carts, buckets, and wringers
(800) 253-9638
roycerolls.net

Franchise and Business Opportunities

Coverall Cleaning Concepts
Coverall North America Inc.
Commercial cleaning
(866) 296-8944
coverall.com

Jani-King International
Commercial cleaning
16885 Dallas Pkwy.
Addison, TX 75001
(972) 991-0900
janiking.com

MaidPro Corp.
77 N. Washington St.
Boston, MA 02114
(888) 624-3776
maidpro.com

The Maids International
9394 W. Dodge Rd., Suite 140
Omaha, NE 68114
(800) 843-6243
maids.com

Molly Maid
3948 Ranchero Dr.
Ann Arbor, MI 48108
(800) 665-5962
mollymaid.com

ServiceMaster Co.
Residential and commercial cleaning, other service franchises
860 Ridge Lake Bl.
Memphis, TN 38120

(901) 597-1400
servicemaster.com

Swisher Hygiene Co.
Restroom hygiene
4725 Piedmont Row Dr., #400
Charlotte, NC 28210
(877) 7SWISHER
swisheronline.com

Internet and Government Resources

CleanLink
Information resource for sanitary supply distributors, building service contractors, and in-house cleaning professionals
cleanlink.com

CleanOutlook
Web and logo design for cleaning companies
cleanoutlook.com

Occupational Safety & Health Administration
osha.gov

Salary.com
On-demand data and software related to employee compensation
salary.com

U.S. Department of Labor
dol.gov

U.S. Patent and Trademark Office
uspto.gov

Magazines and Publications

Note: All books listed are available on Amazon.com

Cleanfax
Carpet care and disaster restoration
NTP Media
19 British American Blvd., W.

Latham, NY 12110
(518) 783-1281
cleanfax.com

***Cleaning & Maintenance Management* magazine**
NTP Media
19 British American Blvd., W.
Latham, NY 12110
(518) 783-1281
cmmonline.com

***Cleaning Business* magazine**
3693 E. Marginal Way, S.
Seattle, WA 98134
(206) 682-9748
cleaningbusiness.com

Construction Cleanup: A Guide to an Exciting & Profitable Cleaning Specialty
Don Aslett
Marsh Creek Press
(888) 748-3535

Don Aslett's Stainbuster's Bible: The Complete Guide to Spot Removal
Don Aslett
Plume
(888) 748-3535

The Cleaning Encyclopedia
Don Aslett
Dell

Entrepreneur's Almanac: Fundamentals, Facts and Figures You Need to Run and Grow Your Business
Jacquelyn Lynn
Entrepreneur Press
entrepreneurpress.com

Green Cleaning for Dummies
Stephen Ashkin and David Holly
greencleaningfordummies.com

How to Clean Windows Like the Pros
John Baxter

How to Upgrade and Motivate Your Cleaning Crews
Don Aslett

Marsh Creek Press
(888) 748-3535

Successful Cleaning Services

AAA Prestige Carpet and Tile Care
Mike Blair
St. George, UT
(435) 652-3736

Biotrauma Inc.
Ryan Sawyer and Benjamin Lichtenwalner
999 Chestnut St.
Gainesville, GA 30501
(770) 262-7206
biotrauma.com

Pro Building Services Inc.
Michael W. Ray, CBSE
1015 South 3600 West
Salt Lake City, UT 84104
(801) 531-6800

Glossary

Attached cushion: a cushioning material, such as foam, rubber, urethane, etc., adhered to the backing fabric side of a carpet to provide additional dimensional stability, thickness, and padding.

Backing: materials (fabrics or yarns) comprising the back of the carpet as opposed to the carpet pile, or face.

Biological hazard (biohazard): an organism or substance derived from an organism that poses a threat to human health; can include substances harmful to animals.

Bleeding: transfer of fiber dyes from carpet or other fabrics by a liquid, usually water, with subsequent redepositing on other fibers.

Blend: a mixture of two or more fibers or yarns.

Carpet cushion: a term used to describe any kind of material placed under carpet to provide softness and adequate support when it is walked on.

CBSE: Certified Building Service Executive, a designation awarded by the Building Service Contractors Association International.

Degreaser: a cleaner designed to remove oils and greases.

Disinfectants/disinfecting: killing microorganisms (bacteria, viruses, fungi) with a chemical agent; many disinfectants are safe and commonly available, some are toxic and damaging to surfaces.

Dry cleaning: a cleaning process that uses chemicals rather than water; dry cleaning isn't necessarily done without moisture.

Dry compound cleaner: carpet cleaning preparation consisting of absorbent granules impregnated with dry cleaning fluids, detergents, and other cleaners; dry powder is sprinkled on the carpet, worked into the pile with a brush, left to absorb soil for a short time, then removed with the absorbed soil by vacuuming.

Environmental Protection Agency (EPA): U.S. government agency responsible for setting and administering air and water standards.

Fastness: retention of color by carpet or other materials.

Occupational Safety & Health Administration (OSHA): U.S. government agency that oversees laws requiring employers to provide employees with a workplace free of hazardous conditions.

Resellers' permits: state Department of Revenue–issued permits that allow you to purchase items you intend to resell without paying sales tax; you're responsible for collecting and remitting sales tax on those items when they're sold.

Rug: carpet cut into room or area dimensions and loose–laid.

Soil retardant: chemical used to help textile fibers resist soiling.

Solvent: any liquid capable of dissolving other liquids or solids; in cleaning, it generally means one of the volatile petroleum or plant distillates used to dissolve oily and greasy soils.

Spot–clean: cleaning a small portion of an object—typically carpet, furniture, or walls—rather than the entire item.

Stripping: process of removing numerous applications of floor finishes (or wax) from hard–surface flooring.

Wet–clean: a cleaning process using water and detergents or soaps.

Index

A

AAA Prestige Carpet Care, 4,
11, 60, 92, 111, 140, 176–177
accidents, responsibility and
reporting, 32–33, 164–165
accountant/accounting, 99, 110,
112
advertising, 156. *See also* marketing
printed, 158
advisory boards, 99–100
agreements, customer, 29. *See
also* contracts
air quality, indoor, 42
answering machine/voice mail,
150
apartment and condominium
cleaning, 18, 19, 22
appearance. *See also* image
importance of, 3
at trade shows, 162

applicants, job, 125, 127–128.
See also employees
screening, 136
asset protection, 95
associations, 164, 169–171
Association of Specialists in
Cleaning and Restoration,
77
attitude, importance of,
124–125
attorney, needs for, 97–98, 136,
142

B

balance sheet, 110
Bane-Clene Corp., 155, 157
bankers, dealing with, 98
Better Business Bureau, 141
billing, 111–113
biohazards, in post death and
trauma cleaning, 81

▲

Blair, Mike, 4, 8, 11, 60, 62, 63, 66, 69, 92, 111, 125, 129, 130, 140, 155, 156, 158, 160
Biotrauma Inc., 81, 177
blind cleaning, 77–78
bonding, 101. *See also* insurance
booths, trade show, 162
Buckets & Bows Maid Service Inc., 33
building cleaning workers, numbers of, 5
business(es). *See also* company; startup
  buying existing, 12–14
  consultants, 99
  image/appearance, 3
  licenses, 118
  office in executive suite, 122
  opportunities, 173–174
  repeat, 10
  seasonal, 11
  setting up, 117
  skills needed, 10
  structuring, 91
  business cards, 122
business plan, 83–87

C

cancellation policies, 29
carpet cleaning, 2, 9, 11, 42, 52, 59, 64, 70, 154
  chemicals, 64–65
  customer complaints, 66–67
  employees, 126, 129
  equipment, 61–62
  invoicing, 69–70, 71
  labor and materials cost, 109
  marketing for, 161
  methods, 63–64
  overhead costs, 109–110
  prices, setting, 109–110
  procedure, 68–69
  profits, 110
  referrals in marketing, 69

technicians, 130
  vehicles and insurance, 120
Carpet and Rug Institute, 72
cash flow statement, 111
ceiling cleaning, 79–80
charges, suggested, for specific cleaning items, 106
chemicals
  carpet cleaning, 64–65, 140
  safe use of, 44, 165
child labor laws, 133–135
chimney sweeping, 79
Cleaning for a Reason Foundation and website, 33
cleaning services
  benefits of, 130
  demand for, 2
  part-time or full-time, 4
  successful, 176–177
  workers, numbers of, 2
commercial cleaners, 1–2
  facility/office, 119
  janitorial, 40
  outsourcing, 3
  security threats and reporting, 13
communicating with market, 155–158
company/companies. *See also*
  business(es); business plan
  naming, 92–93
  organization, 85
  successful, 155
competition, 2, 86, 165
  for carpet cleaning services, 60–61, 86
  for janitorial services, 41–42, 86
  for residential cleaning, 19, 86
computer
  and printer, 146
  bookkeeping software, 112
  experts, 99
  skills, 166
  spreadsheet program, 166

consultants, business, 99, 171
consumer markets, 1, 2. *See also* market
contracts
    janitorial, 10, 49
    residential cleaning, 10
    with vendors, 142
conventions/exhibitions, 11, 160. *See also*
    trade shows
corporation, as business option, 94, 95
costs, startup
    for carpet cleaners, 65
    for janitorial services, 40
    for residential cleaners, 16
    for window cleaners, 77
Crawford, Jerry, 13
credit and debit policies/equipment/
    sources, 113–114, 148, 172–173
creditors, 143. *See also* supplies; suppliers
crews. *See* team cleaning
custodians, 44. *See also* janitorial service
customers
    agreement form, 28
    complaints
    carpet cleaning, 66–67
    janitorial, 44
    information forms, 26, 29, 36
    problem, 30–31
    prospective/target, 26–27, 95, 107,
        154
    records / file, 29–30, 48
    repeat, 10–11
    residential, 16–17, 18, 157
customer service/satisfaction, 166
    carpet cleaning, 67–68, 69
    janitorial, 44, 47, 54, 126
    as marketing tool, 156

D

damage report and form, 29, 32, 37
deliveries, 101, 102
demographic analysis, 155

disaster cleaning and restoration, 4, 77
distributors, 141, 142
doorknob hangers, 157
drapes, cleaning, 73
driver's license, 124

E

email, 151
employee(s)
    benefits, 132–133
    driving qualifications and history,
        121–122
    immigrants as, 31
    job application, 124
    hiring, 129
    legality of, 129
    pay, 129
    prospective, 125–127
    recruiting, 124
    supervision, 67, 136
    taking care of, 128–129, 165
    theft, 135–137
    time sheet, residential, 17, 34
    training, 54, 128, 129–132
    turnover, 41, 54, 63, 125
    vehicles and insurance for, 120
Employment Eligibility Verification
    Form, 129
EPA regulations, 81
equipment, 145, 146, 148, 159. *See also*
    supplies
    and tools, 119
    for carpet and upholstery cleaning, 62
    for janitorial services, 42–44, 47, 54
    for residential cleaning, 19, 20, 21
    for window cleaning, 76
    secondhand, 150
    storage, 118
estimating
    carpet cleaning, 67–68
    computers used in, 146

janitorial prices, 50–53
residential prices, 26–28
exhibits, 161. *See also* trade shows
experience, importance of, 163

F

Fair Labor Standards Act, 134, 135
fax machine/service, 147
feather dusters, 23
fee schedule, 98
financial
    advisor, 99
    projections, 85
    statements, 143
flexibility, need for, 4, 26
floor cleaning
    residential, 42–43
    janitorial instructions, 51–52
food services industry, janitorial services
    for, 41
freight and freight costs, 102, 141
franchise(s), 173–174
    uniforms, 132
    vs. independent operation, 12, 19
furniture inspection and cleaning, 70,
    72–73

G

geographical area served, 154, 158
gift certificates, 157
government programs, for small busi-
    ness support, 104–105
Guzman, Wanda/Guzman Commercial
    Cleaning, 3, 9, 27, 107, 128

H

health concerns, 41, 45
HEPA filters, 42
holiday scheduling for residential serv-
    ices, 31–32
homebased services/offices, 11, 117–118
    carpet cleaning, 60

janitorial, 40
residential, 16, 107–108
tax advantage of, 118–119
honesty, as requirement, 9, 100
hospitals, janitorial services in, 40
housecleaning services, 3, 15, 17. *See also*
    residential cleaning services
human resources, 99, 122–123. *See also*
    employees
    job description, 124

I

image/appearance, 159, 162
Incomm Research Center, 160
independent operations/contractors, 12,
    19, 47
insurance, 101, 159
    agent, 98, 101
    company claims, 33
    for drivers, 121–122
    for janitorial service, 54
    for residential service, 120
internet
    access, 146–147, 158
    resources, 175
inventory and inventory control, 140,
    146
invoices / billing, 112–113

J

Jani–King International Inc, 13
janitorial service, 2, 9, 11, 39–40, 60
    bidding, 49–50, 53, 109
    billing, 54
    cash flow, 54–55
    complaints, handling, 44–45
    contracts, 10, 49
    employees for, 126
    equipment and supplies, 42–44, 47,
        54
    estimating, 50–53, 57 (form)

labor and materials cost, 108
laundry facility for, 48
mission statement, 87
overhead costs, 108–109
prices, setting, 108–109
profits, 109
proposal form, 58
quarterly master plan, 48
researching, 154
references, 54
security, keys, and safety, 54,
    55–56
standard operations, 44–48
task times, 49
training, 128
vehicles and insurance, 120
wet and dry work, 47
Jones, Waldo, Holbrook & McDonough
    law firm, 136

K

keys, how to handle, 31, 54
Konopacki, Allen, 160

L

labor, costs and cost estimates, 105, 106,
    108–110, 166
lead-exchange group or club, 158
learning, never stop, 164
legal structure/advice, 94–95, 97, 99
licenses/license fees, 95–97, 112, 118
Lichtenwalner, Benjamin, 81
limited liability company (LLC), 94

M

magazines, 175–176
maid service, 33, 161
mailing and shipping, 102
management structure, 85
manufacturing/manufacturers
    buying directly from, 141, 142
    facilities, janitorial services for, 40

market
    communicating with, 155–158
    defining, 155
    research, 85–87, 154
marketing, 153
    experts, 99
    and follow-up, 161–162
    message, 156
    plan, 85, 153, 158. *See also* business plan
    to residential customers, 157
    word-of-mouth, 156
markup, calculating, 115
materials, costs. *See* labor
material safety data sheet (MSDS), 65
medical offices, janitorial services for,
    40–41
mission and mission statement, 87–89
model home cleaning, 18
Molly Maid and Ms. Molly Foundation,
    159
multi–function devices, 146
multi–unit residential cleaning, 18, 22

N

naming your company, 92–93
negotiating and negotiating prices, 107
    with suppliers, 143–144
networking, 156, 157
new home cleaning, 18
niche businesses/markets, 3, 5, 9–10, 75,
    154, 165–166

O

O'Brien, Michael P., 136, 137
Occupational Safety & Health
    Administration (OSHA), 65, 78, 81
office(s). *See also* homebased services
    in executive suite, 122
    janitorial services for, 40
office equipment/furnishings, 146–148
    and supply checklist, 149

operating costs, calculation chart, 115

outsourcing painting and carpet cleaning, 18

overhead/overhead rate, 106, 107–110

Owens, Fenna, 8, 9, 23, 107, 157, 164, 165

P

Page, Patti/Page's Personal Cleaning, 27, 105, 114, 177

paper shredder, 148

partnerships, 93, 94, 95, 104

PayPal, 114, 158

permits, 95–97

pets, considerations for, 28

photocopier, 147

pollutants, 79–80

postage scale/meter/stamps, 147–148

post death and trauma cleaning, 81

predictability, 10–11

pressure washing, 4, 47, 78

pricing/prices, policy, setting, and structure, 105

    carpet cleaning, 109–110

    janitorial, 50, 53, 108–109

    residential, 26, 107

printed materials, 159

Privacy Act, 9

problems, dealing with, 165

Pro Building Services Inc., 4, 8, 40, 97, 177

professional services, seeking, 97

profit and loss (P&L) statements, 110

profits/profitability, 107, 108–110, 115, 167

promotion, 26. *See also* marketing

PTO. *See* U.S. Patent and Trademark Office

publications as resources, 175–176

purchasing, 139, 140, 144. *See also* supplies; suppliers

Q

qualifications, 9–10

quality, need for, 2

R

Ray, Michael W., 4, 8, 40, 42, 48, 49, 50, 97, 164, 166

record keeping, 110–111, 137

    on computer, 146

references, checking, 127

referrals, 155, 157

research. *See* market, research

residential cleaning services, 2, 9, 10, 13, 16, 27, 154, 155

    agreements/contracts, 29

    budgets, 167

    checklists, 24, 26, 29, 35

    contracts, 10

    employees for, 126

    equipment, 19, 20, 21

    estimating/quoting, 26–28

    holiday scheduling, 31–32

    homebased, 16, 107–108

    labor and materials cost, 108

    marketing to, 157

    mission statement, 87

    overhead costs, 107–108

    payment, 27

    pitfalls and challenges, 30–31

    prices, setting, 107–108

    profits, 109

    prospective customers, 16–17

    records, maintaining customer, 28–30

    scheduling, 25

    security and keys, 31

    skills needed, 9–10

    supplies and costs, 21–22

    system for cleaning, 26

    time sheets, 17, 34

    typical day, 25–26

vehicles and insurance, 120
resources, tapping, 164
restaurants, as market, 4, 40, 45
restroom cleaning, 78–79
retail stores, janitorial services for, 40
role modeling, 131

S
safety
    driving, 121
    equipment and precautions, 44, 78
salespeople, 141. *See also* suppliers
sandblasting, 47
Sardone, Deborah, 33
schools, janitorial services for, 40
seasonality of services, 11
security
    for janitorial service, 54, 55–56
    keys and, 31
    systems, 136
    threats and reporting, 13
shredders, paper, 148
shipping, 102
single-family residents, cleaning for, 22
smocks, 132
social networking, 151–152
software, 146
sole proprietorships, 93, 94, 95
specialty services, 75. *See also* niche busi-
    nesses
spring cleaning, 32
square feet
    calculating for carpet cleaning, 69,
        111
    cleaned per hour (table), 46
startup and costs, 85, 104–105
    carpet cleaning, 60, 65
    janitorial, 40, 55
    residential cleaning, 8, 16
    window cleaning, 77
state taxes and licenses, 96, 97

storage, 102, 118, 119
subcontracting, 23
supplies, 145
    buying, 141–142
    checklist, 149
    for janitorial service, 53, 108–109
    for residential cleaners, 21–22
    sources, 172–173
    storage for, 118
suppliers. *See also* vendors
    choosing, 140
    dealing/negotiating with, 143–144
    representatives, 141
systems, developing, 164

T
taxes
    business, 112
    homebase advantage in, 118–119
    payroll, 112
    reporting, 125
    sales, 96
team cleaning
    janitorial, 46–47
    residential, 23
telecommunications, 148–151
telephone/cell phone, 149, 150
    used in marketing, 154
toll-free number, 151
trademarks, 93–94
trade shows, 11, 160–162
Trade Show Week Show Directory, 160

U
uniforms, 54, 132, 133
upholstery cleaning, 59, 62. *See also* car-
    pet cleaning
U.S. Department of Labor, 134
U.S. Patent and Trademark Office
    (PTO), 93
U.S. Postal Service, 148

V

vacuum cleaners/cleaning, 40, 42, 43

vehicles, 20, 119–121, 159

vendors, 140, 142, 144. *See also* suppliers

    carpet cleaning, 62

    contracts, 142

    payment terms with, 144

W

wages/wage scale, 135

wall cleaning, 79–80

warehouses, janitorial services for, 40

waste handling, 41

water damage restoration, 66

websites/web page, 158

    design, 99

    residential services, 86

    trade show, 160

window cleaning, 2, 4, 53, 76–78, 80

Work Experience and Career
    Exploration Program, 134